POR

Happy Hour
GUIDEBOOK

2007 EDITION

Portland Happy Hour Guidebook

First Edition

Cindy Anderson

ISBN: 978-0-9791201-0-7

All research, reviews, illustrations, maps and design by Cindy Anderson

Cover photo by A.L. Spangler

Printing by Encore Graphics; Beaverton, OR

Due to the fluid nature of the ever-changing Portland Happy Hour scene, Half-Full Enterprises cannot accept responsibility for any complications that may arise from using the information in this book. Every effort has been made to maintain accuracy, but things change, and Half-Full Enterprises cannot guarantee that the information in this book is or will be accurate. The opinions expressed in this book are just that, opinions of the author. The author did not receive any endorsement earnings (or bribes!) from any bar/restaurant/tavern in the writing of this book. Finally, you are responsible for your own actions, before, during and after using the information provided in this book. Drink responsibly!!! Half-Full Enterprises is not liable for any irresponsible actions on your part, including but not limited to drunk dialing, hooking up with an ex-boyfriend or girlfriend, hurting yourself or hurting someone else.

Half-Full Enterprises

10350 N. Vancouver Way, Suite 173

Portland, OR 97217

www.happyhourguidebook.com

email: cindy@happyhourguidebook.com

Dedication

It is with true appreciation that I honor the sacrifices and hardships my friends have endured in the name of Margaritas!

Biggest and best-est thanks to
Angela Wright, Ed Querfeld, and Chrys Pappas
for their relentless dedication to the cause, rock-solid support, and intrepid tavern-traveling! I love you guys!

Special thanks to Celinda Shannon who took me to my very first Portland Happy Hour and later joined me for many, many more; to Tom Thompson, who in a conversation at Kell's said, "You should write a Happy Hour book!"; to Nell Johnson for her insightful editing help; and to Julee Wasserman who coached me in actually getting all this done.

AND a great-full shout-out to my "research assistants" who accompanied me on my quest (in order of appearance): Celinda and the "FOCs": Karen, Ellie, Sara, Bridget, Alison, Tom, and Nell; my most special MasterMind sisters Angela, Nicole, and Marlene; Captain Ed and the whole MiPL group; Tonya, Wonderful Chrys, Steve, Joey, Mardell, Julee, The SwizzleChix, Sherrie, Mary & Mary; my fellow Happy Hour Queens Suzanne, Kari, and Jillian; plus Dawnie, Ellie & Aaron, Diane, Tara, Kathy & Jeff, Amy, Dayan, Christi, Cassy, Vonnie, Will, Lisa, and Mike. Further gratitude goes to the Ladies Who Launch group and my Incubator family. And to all my Illinois loved ones – you are always with me in spirit(s)!

XOXO

"To all my friends!"

– Mickey Rourke in *Barfly*

"One of the secrets
of a happy life is
continuous small treats."

– Iris Murdoch –

Contents

"Follow your bliss."

– Joseph Campbell –

Maps

Portland Map Areas

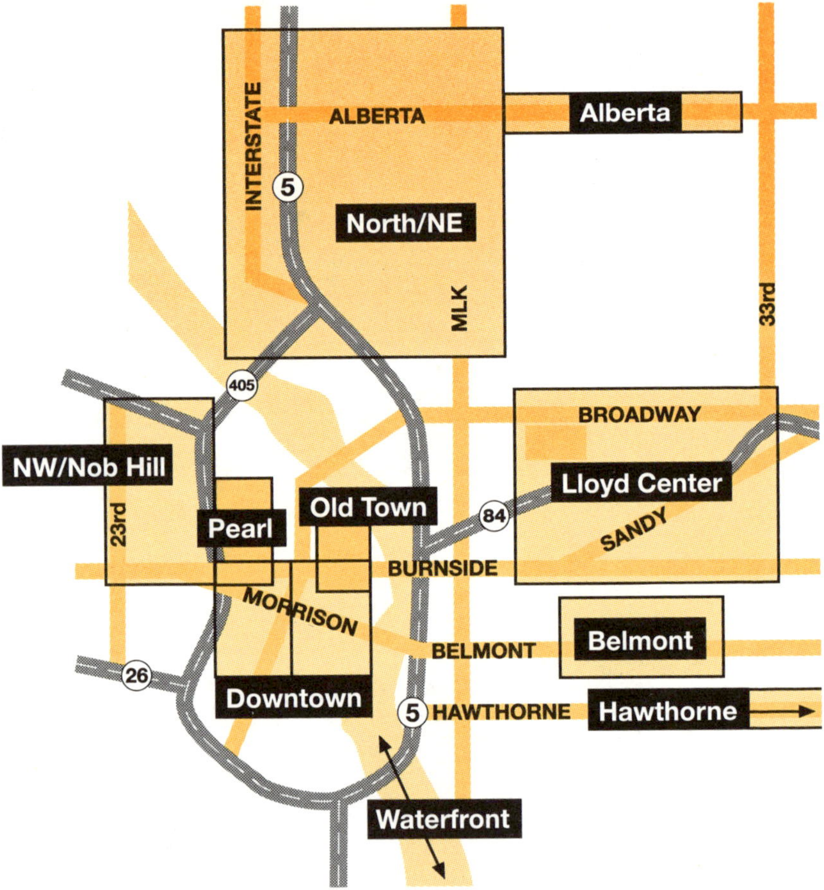

Restaurant Locations

- Indicates a full review in alphabetical listings
- Mentioned elsewhere, but not fully reviewed

Map Area Page

Alberta

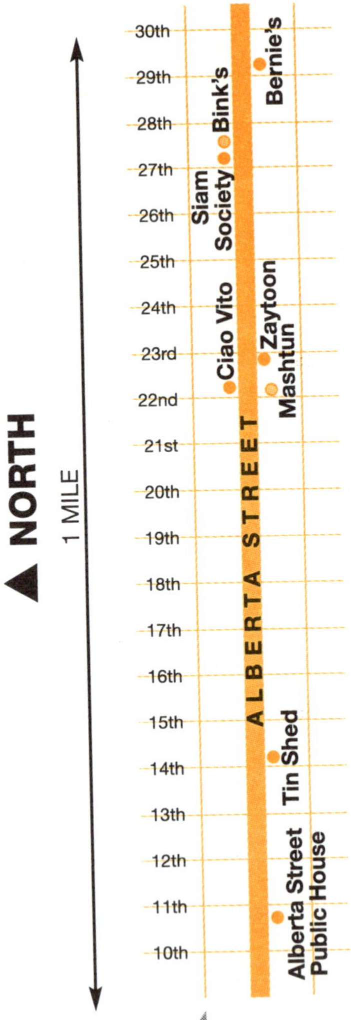
NORTH
1 MILE
ALBERTA STREET
30th
29th
28th
27th
26th
25th
24th
23rd
22nd
21st
20th
19th
18th
17th
16th
15th
14th
13th
12th
11th
10th
Bernie's
Bink's
Siam Society
Ciao Vito
Zaytoon
Mashtun
Tin Shed
Alberta Street Public House

Belmont Area

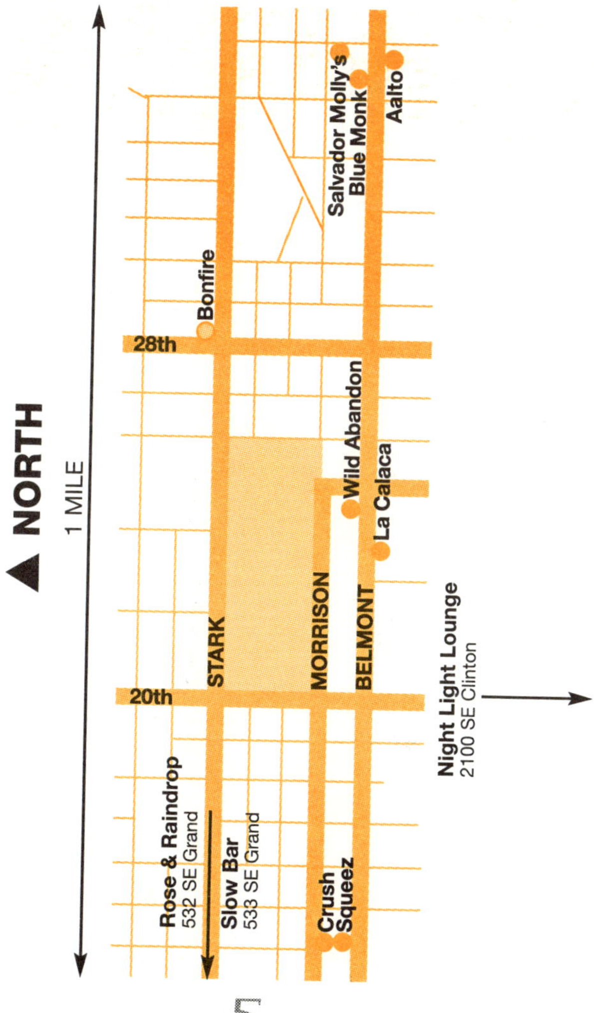

Downtown-West

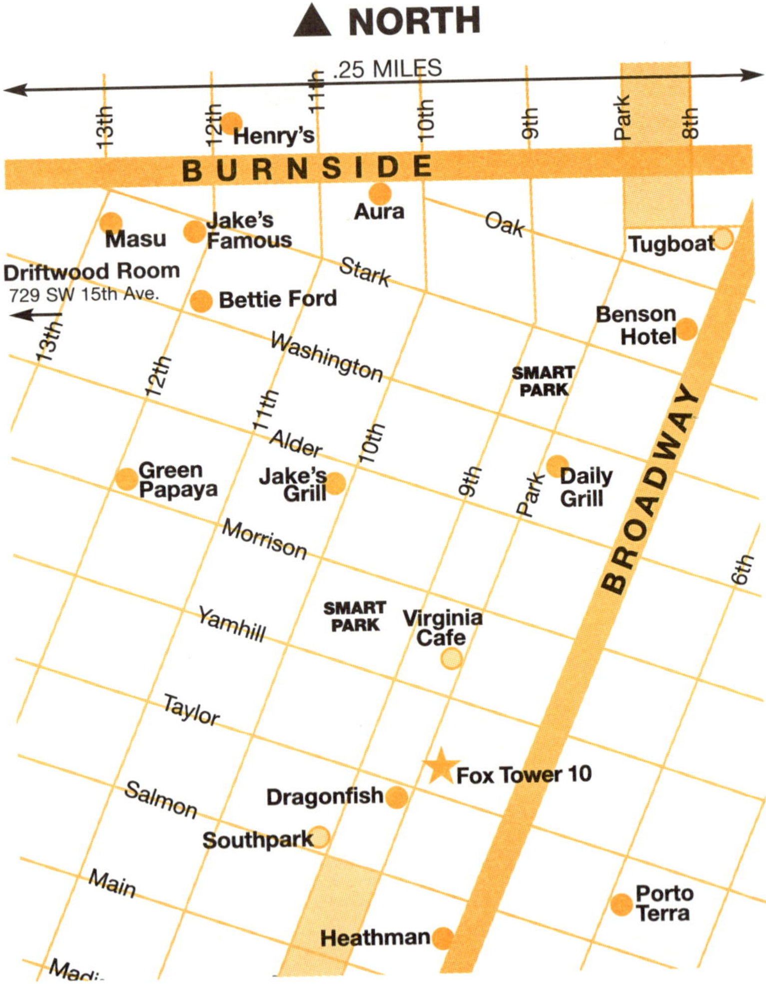

Downtown–East

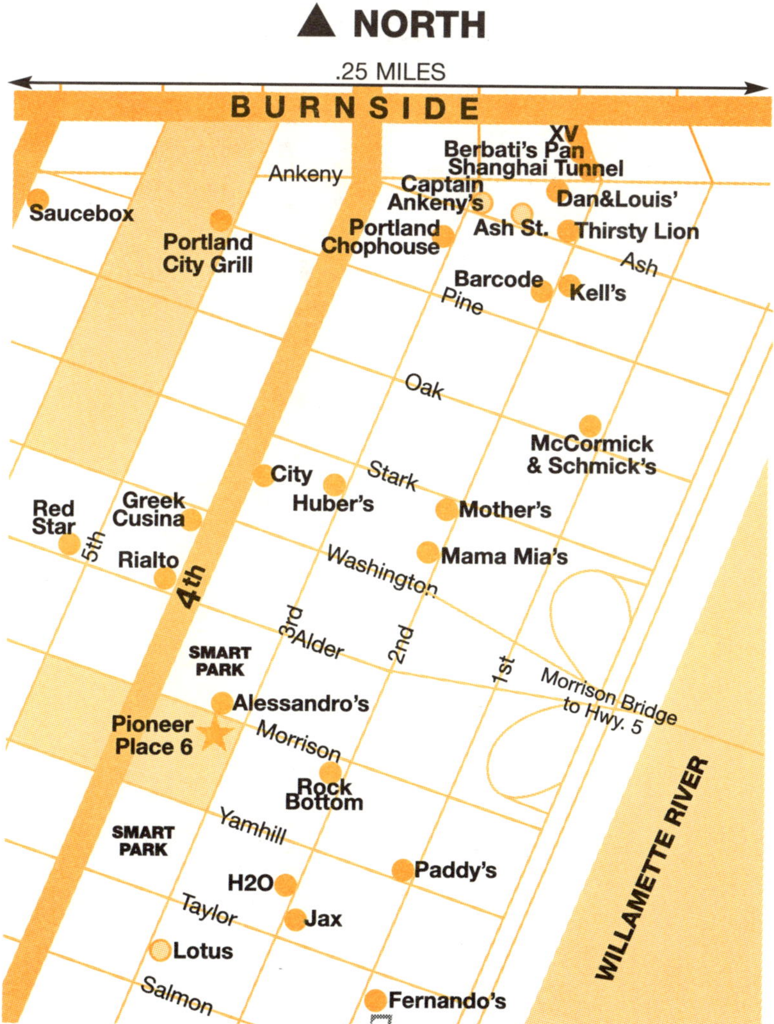

Hawthorne

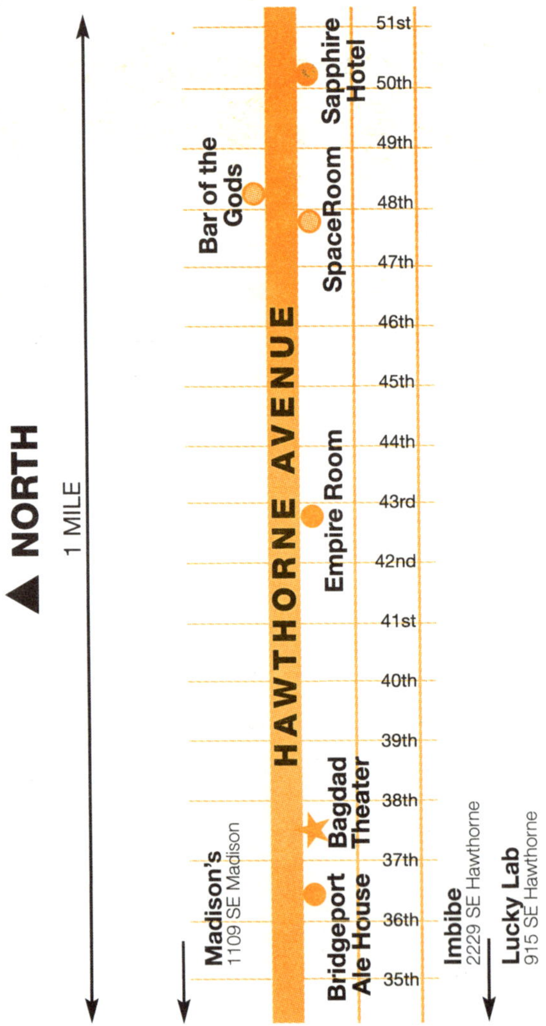
NORTH
1 MILE
HAWTHORNE AVENUE
51st
50th
49th
48th
47th
46th
45th
44th
43rd
42nd
41st
40th
39th
38th
37th
36th
35th
Sapphire Hotel
Bar of the Gods
SpaceRoom
Empire Room
Bagdad Theater
Bridgeport Ale House
Madison's
1109 SE Madison
Imbibe
2229 SE Hawthorne
Lucky Lab
915 SE Hawthorne

Lloyd Center-ish

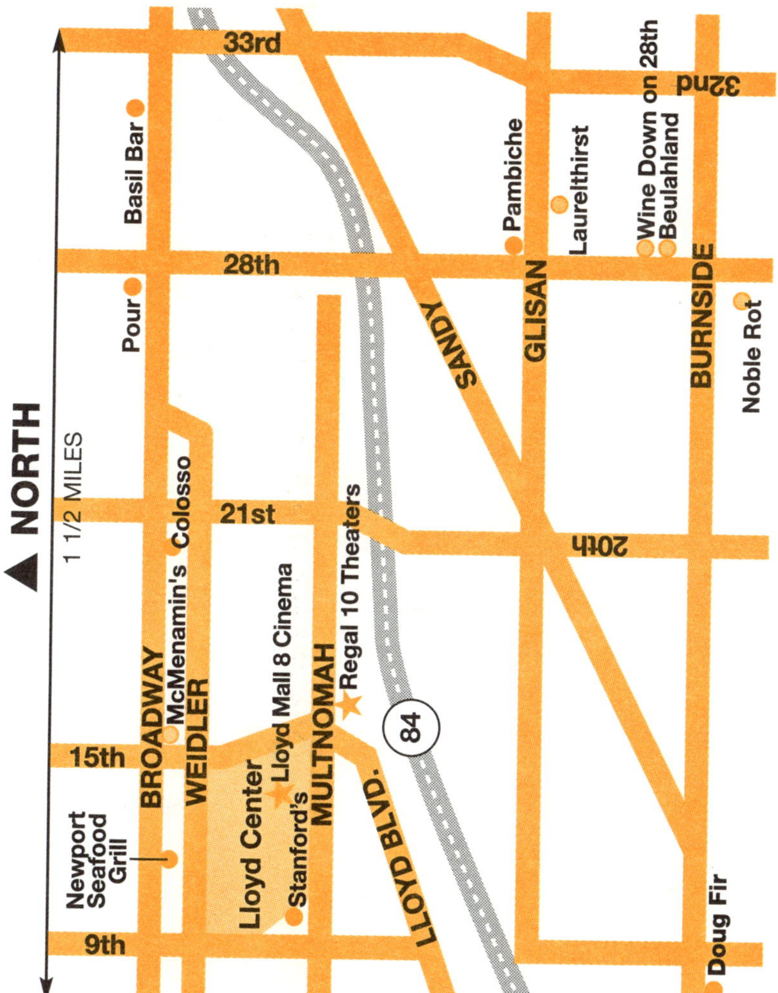

North/NE

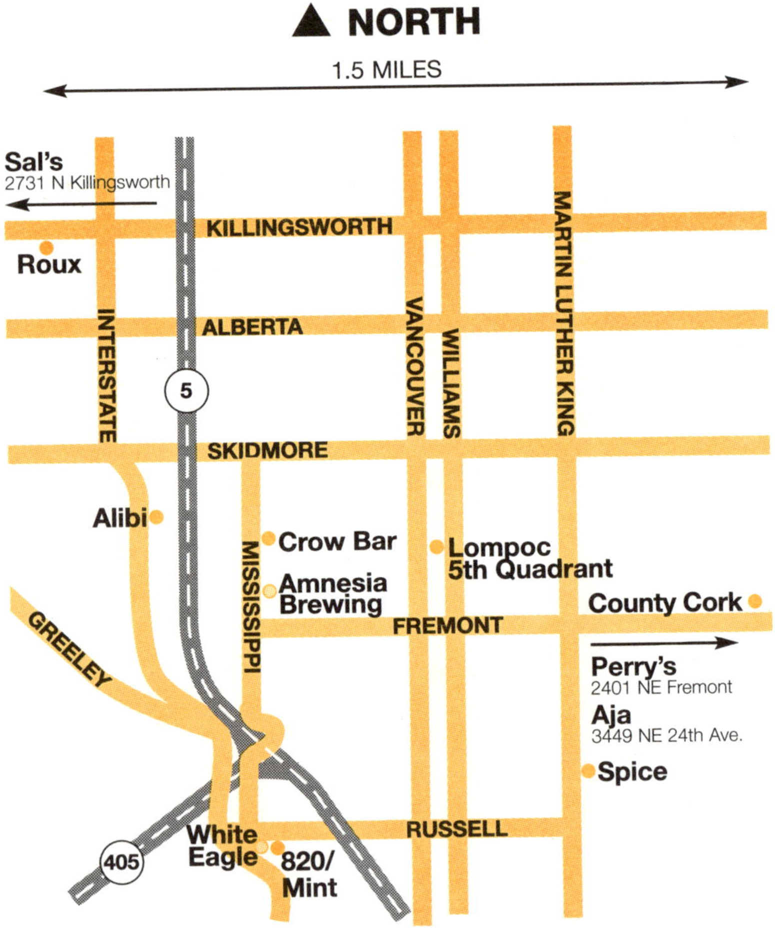
NORTH
1.5 MILES
Sal's
2731 N Killingsworth
KILLINGSWORTH
Roux
ALBERTA
INTERSTATE
5
VANCOUVER
WILLIAMS
MARTIN LUTHER KING
SKIDMORE
Alibi
Crow Bar
Lompoc
5th Quadrant
Amnesia
Brewing
MISSISSIPPI
County Cork
GREELEY
FREMONT
Perry's
2401 NE Fremont
Aja
3449 NE 24th Ave.
Spice
RUSSELL
White
Eagle
820/
Mint
405

NW / Nob Hill

21st/23rd

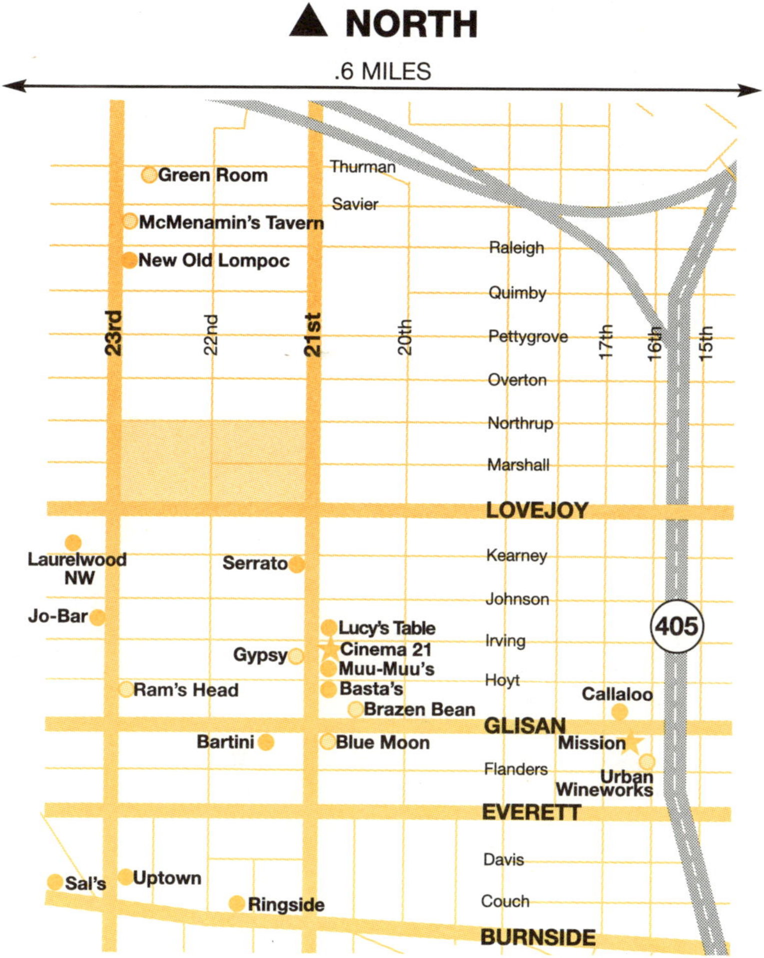

Old Town

a.k.a. "Happy Hour Heaven"

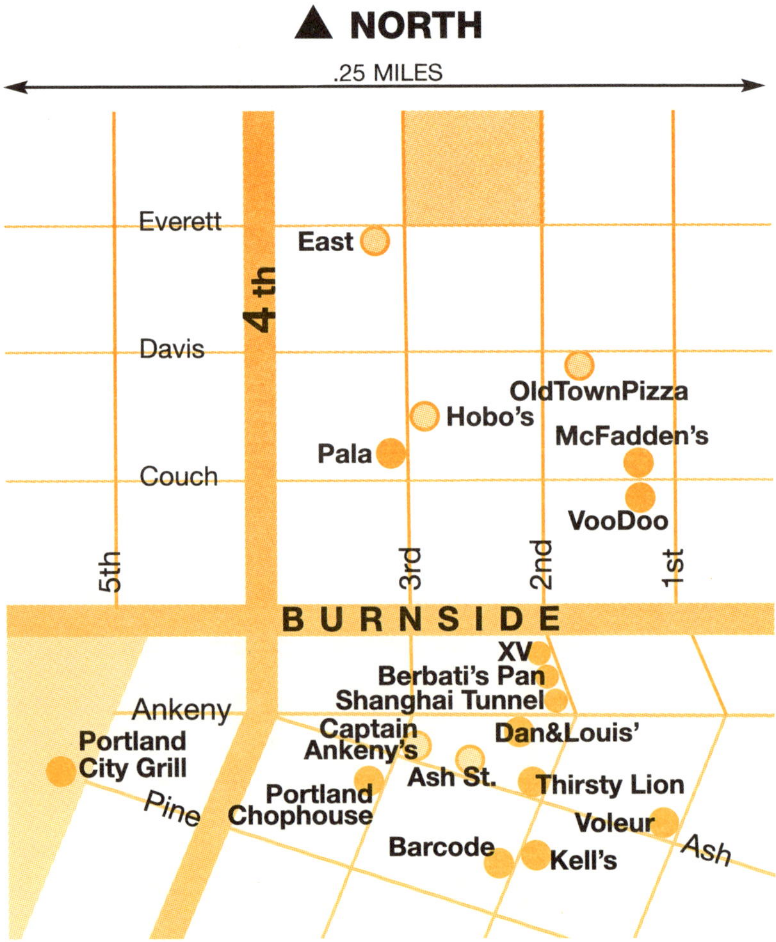

Pearl District

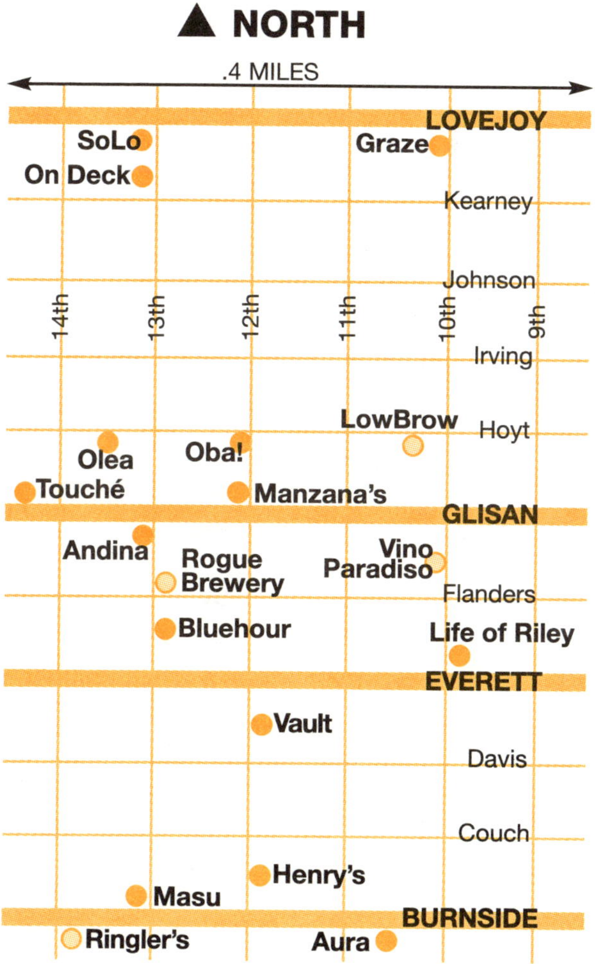

Waterfront

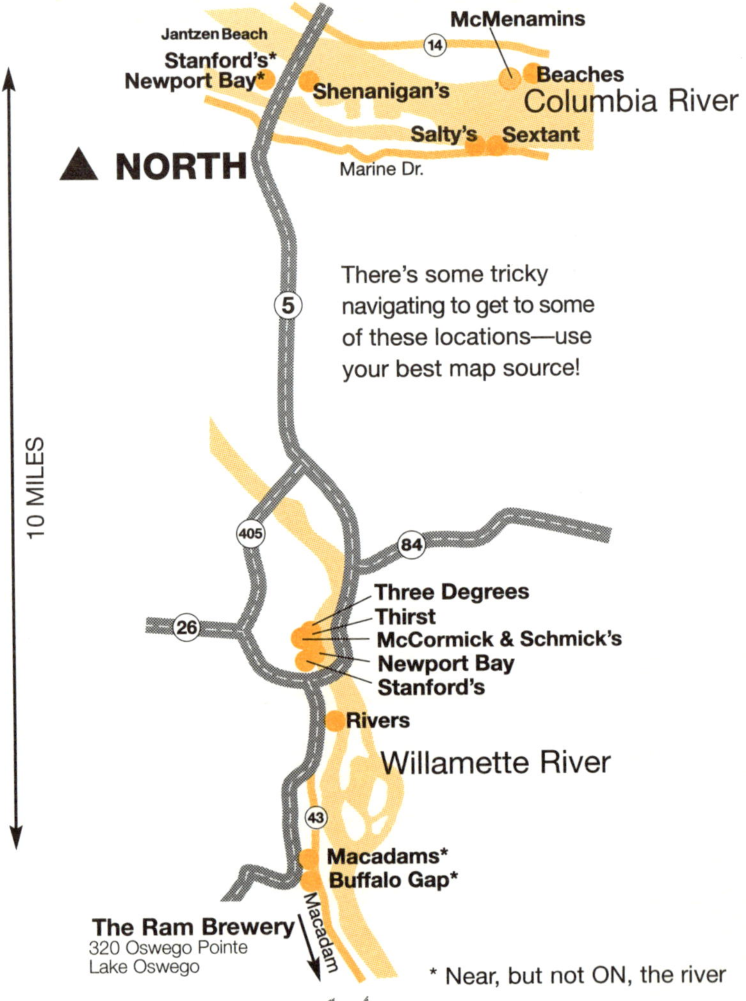

There's some tricky navigating to get to some of these locations—use your best map source!

* Near, but not ON, the river

Listings

Notes & Disclaimers

Accuracy of information: Things change! Graciously accept this fluidity and adjust your attitude accordingly. As of this writing, the information herein is current. Every effort has been made to present information accurately.

Crowd scene: An element that can greatly vary. I elected not to try to qualify the type of person typically visiting a certain place, but rather encourage you to reserve judgement as well and be accepting and tolerant—and even friendly—to your fellow bar patrons. Also, please be aware that the more popular places get crowded. Be flexible, prompt, and patient. Hopefully this book will encourage you to get out there and EXPLORE! Every place in this book is worth checking out.

Service: I didn't comment on this aspect as "one bad apple doesn't spoil the whole bunch." Be aware that sometimes it's service via bartender only. Be proactive yet polite.

Tipping: Servers may have to make just as many trips for you as a regular diner. Please consider the effort—not the totally LOW bill—and be extra-generous for good service!

Rating & Judging: All judging is based on HAPPY HOUR only. You may find you have different opinions of places. I called 'em as I saw 'em. TAKE YOUR OWN NOTES for future reference throughout the book. Record your adventures within and it can be a fun walk down Memory Lane...

Do NOT drink and drive!!! Ever.

Happy Hours often relegated to bar area only. Mostly, I've commented on the entire restaurant atmosphere overall, including outdoor seating (which may not always be available to the Happy Hour crowd). Ask before you are seated to confirm available service.

FOOD

About Food Ratings

Food Deals

1 = **Limited food alternatives**
A place could have sub-par food, but more than likely a "one" rating means a limited menu, small portions, or a meager price break during Happy Hour compared to other times of the day.

2 = **Pretty decent deals and/or selections**
Places rated with a "two" offer basic good food at lower Happy Hour prices. Most places will fall into this category.

3 = **Exceptionally delicious and discounted**
These are restaurants that kind of "blow the curve" for everyone else. They offer lots of different menu choices with many sizable portions AND their food is exceptionally tasty.

About Drink Ratings

Drink Specials

0 = **No drink discount**
Sadly, not every bar/restaurant offers drink discounts at Happy Hour (which technically goes against the definition of the term); however, they make us quite happy with their food. And hey, if you don't want to drink, it makes no difference.

1 = **Limited drink selection and/or discount**
Only one point for bars not offering much of a discount or many drink options.

2 = **Pretty decent deals and/or selections**
For basic, but probably limited drink specials.

3 = **Extra-cheap drinks and/or several alternatives**
A "three" is for bars offering an extra-big discount, unique options or have great specials on beer, wine AND wells.

About Atmosphere

Atmosphere

1 = **Very basic/nothing special**
Sometimes it's like the owners didn't put much thought into decorating. They get "ones" here.

2 = **Casual style**
A nice place, but design concept not taken far.

3 = **Upscale, unusual decor or nice view**
Wow! These places "knocked my socks off"! Reflects a creative effort that enhances the customer's experience.

Overall, I didn't address how crowded bars are. Some of the best places were quite empty, which is unbelievable to me. People of Portland: Get out there and ENJOY! Try new spots—you can enjoy a nice restaurant meal for a fraction of dinner prices!

7

Waterfront

BIG number indicates overall rating/score

Indicates which map

A white star indicates places that would be perfect except they don't offer drink specials

Food Deals	2
Drink Specials	+ 2
Atmosphere	+ 2
	= 7?

Magic Point!

A note about the "Magic Point" System:

The "magic point" is an arbitrary point that I sometimes threw into the final score to account for the synergistic effect of the whole being greater than the sum of its parts. I chose to use only *whole numbers* when rating each category of food, drink or atmosphere, and since I didn't use half-points, sometimes the tallied score just didn't quite do the bar justice. Plus I wanted some places to get perfect "10"s.

Okay, so now the fun starts...

9

North/NE

820 N Russell
(503) 460-0820
www.mintrestaurant.com

820/Mint

Happy Hours 4:00–6:30pm Mon–Sat

Food Deals 2 $2.50–$6.00
It's all about the sweet potato fries!
Limited but delicious, unique menu:
lamb burger, calamari, soup & salad

Drink Specials 3 $3.00 well drinks
$2.50 draft beers
$5.00 selected cocktails (yum!)

Atmosphere 3 Connected to the gorgeous & hip Mint Restaurant; trendy, upscale ultra-lounge; nice back deck area where you can pleasantly enjoy Happy Hour on a nice day.

Extra Info Known for their famous Lucy Signature Cocktail Creations

7

Belmont Area

3356 SE Belmont
(503) 235-6041

Aalto

Happy Hours 4:00–7:00pm Daily

Food Deals 3 $2.00–$5.00
Big AND delicious portions: steak, meatball, ham & cheese or grilled veggie sandwiches; fresh greens or Caesar salad, stuffed mushrooms, crostini

Drink Specials 2 $1.00 off drafts and wells

Atmosphere 2 Compelling and retro-y with an artsy vibe, subtle funkiness, and loungy ambience. Check out the back patio on a nice day!

7

North/NE

3449 NE 24th Ave.
(503) 287-5400

Aja Pacific House

Happy Hours	4:00–7:00pm Daily
Food Deals 2	$2.00 Mmmm...scallop cigars (a.k.a. egg rolls), beef skewers, soup, wasabi tots, mixed greens
Drink Specials 3	$1.00 domestic special $2.50 micros & well drinks $3.00 selected wine
Atmosphere 2	Down-played neutrals in homey wood-walled open room; slight Asian (aja-n) touches; art pieces; chalkboard specials at big bar; nice & quiet; sidewalk seating.
Extra Info	Private small group room provides quiet seating for 8–10

7

Alberta

1036 NE Alberta
(503) 284-7665

Alberta St. Public House

Happy Hours 5:00–8:00pm Mon–Fri

Food Deals 3 $3.00
Basic but big: turkey sandwich, Guiness beef stew, mixed greens salad, nachos, BLT, fries, veggie melt, chicken sandwich

Drink Specials 3 $1.00 PBRs
$2.50 micros
$2.75 wells
$2.75 selected wine

Atmosphere 2 If the music isn't blaring, and the candles are all aglow, its a delight to walk into this very warm and inviting, dark Irish pub. Booths have high walls enabling private conversation.

7

North/NE

4024 N Interstate Ave.
(503) 287-5335

Alibi

Happy Hours	3:00–7:00pm Daily
Food Deals 2	$1.95–$2.95 Bar fare with island touches; taco quesadilla, dinner salad, hot wings, soup, onion rings, BBQ cheddar burger with fries
Drink Specials 2	$2.50 tropicals (nightly specials) $1.75 Bud
Atmosphere 3	Top marks for over-the-top tacky Tiki; bizarrely dark & divey; a unique Portland treasure. You really must experience it!
Extra Info	Karoke weekends, Saturday midnight buffet, party specialists

8

Downtown
(East Map)

301 SW Morrison
(503) 222-3900
www.alessandrosrestaurant.com

Alessandro's

Happy Hours 4:00–7:00pm Mon–Sat
All day on Sunday

Food Deals 3 $2.00–$5.50
Penne marinara, pesto linguini, pizza (only $2.00!), calamari, Caesar, minestrone, mozz stix

Drink Specials 2 $2.75 beer
$3.00 wells

Atmosphere 2 Cozy & sweet Italian restaurant, old world charm with arbor-style hangings over the bar, side walls, and interior cafe windows.

7

Pearl

1314 NW Glisan
(503) 228-9535
www.andinarestaurant.com

Andina

Happy Hours	4:00–6:00pm Daily
Food Deals 1	$2.00 Choice of few, but interesting, delicious ethnic small plates: skewers of marinated chicken, beef heart, or grilled octopus
Drink Specials 2	$5.00 Excellent variety of south-of-the-border concoctions including pineapple mojitos
Atmosphere 3	More center-city Lima than Machu Picchu Peruvian; high wooden beamed ceilings, copper-topped tables, painted stucco walls, captivating fireplace.

10

Downtown (West Map)

1022 W Burnside
(503) 597-2872
www.auraportland.com

Aura

Happy Hours	4:30–6:30pm Daily 10:00pm–close Sun–Thurs (food)
Food Deals 3	$2.00–$4.00 Caesar and house salads, wings, hummus plate, fondue, quesadilla, mini burger w/fries, pizza
Drink Specials 3	$3.00 featured wine $3.00 featured draft pints $3.00 martini, Margarita, cosmo, or lemon drop
Atmosphere 3	Enjoy the nightclub atmosphere with hi-tech abstract light screens, white glowing bar, and trapezoid tables in private curtained booths. Don't miss the see-thru stylish bathrooms!

8

Old Town

133 SW 2nd Ave.
(503) 242-0019

Barcode

Happy Hours	4:00–10:00pm Daily (10:00pm!!!!)
Food Deals 3	$1.95–$3.95 Excellent Thai food (connected with E-San Thai Restaurant); 15 offerings including satay, pad thai, skewers, fried rice, fries, garden rolls, Caesar salad, BBQ, egg rolls, fish cakes and wontons
Drink Specials 2	$2.00 & $3.00 well drinks
Atmosphere 2	Hi-tech industrial club look with warm and comfy lounge feel. Dancing later on in tucked away back room.

10

NW/Nob Hill

2108 NW Glisan
(503) 224-7919

Bartini

Happy Hours	4:00–6:30pm Mon–Sat 9:30pm–close Mon–Sat 4:00–close Sunday
Food Deals 3	$2.00–$6.00 Lots of choices including salads, mussels, salmon mousse, soup, mac & cheese, burgers, ahi tuna, saganaki, mushrooms, plus fondues and sampler plate
Drink Specials 3	Half-off house martinis! (menu of 100 martini concoctions)
Atmosphere 3	Black, black and more black (from what I could/couldn't see); small & intimate martini lounge; best appreciated after sunset.

7

Lloyd Center-ish

3135 NE Broadway
(503) 281-8337
www.sweetbasilor.com

Basil Bar

Happy Hours	4:30–6:30pm Mon–Fri 4:30pm–close Sun
Food Deals 3	$2.00–$4.00 WOW! YUM! 14 delicious Thai specials: OMG crab rolls, wraps, calamari salad (award-winning), wings, tom yum & tom kah soup
Drink Specials 1	A few random weekday specials; spendy but unique cocktail list (i.e. raspberry mojito, Thai me up)
Atmosphere 2	Out of a Thai IKEA showroom; large screen TV with couches; mysterious lounge-y back room.
Extra Info	Attached Sweet Basil's back garden area is SWEET!

8

NW/Nob Hill

410 NW 21st Ave.
(503) 274-1572
www.bastastrattoria.citysearch.com

Basta's Trattoria

Happy Hours	5:00–6:30pm
Food Deals 3	$3.00 Unusual samplings including carpaccio, antipasto, Caesar, calamari, chicken skewers with sweet potato fries, polenta
Drink Specials 3	$3.00 beers $3.00 red or white wine $3.00 drink-of-the-day
Atmosphere 2	Retro Italian on the down-low with high-up mural paintings; kidney shapes and velvet drapes; outdoor sidewalk seating

8

Waterfront

919 SE Columbia River Dr.
Vancouver, WA • (360) 699-1592
www.beachesrestaurantandbar.com

Beaches

Happy Hours	4:00–6:00pm Daily 10:00pm–11:00pm Tues–Sat 9:00–10:00pm Sun & Mon
Food Deals 2	$1.95-$3.95 Several pizzas and salads, wings, soups, quesadilla, DESSERTS!
Drink Specials 2	$2.95 beer plus nightly special
Atmosphere 3	Yes, it's out of Portland boundaries, but its still close and SOO nice along the river there! Fun but refined beach bar motif, wall-to-wall giant windows, and fireplace. Good in combo with Vancouver's Cinetopia.
Extra info	Traffic over the Hwy. 5 bridge can take a l-o-n-g time. You might want to hit this early or on weekends if coming from the south.

Downtown
(West Map)

309 SW Broadway
(503) 228-2000
www.bensonhotel.com

7 The Benson

Happy Hours	3:00–7:00pm Mon–Fri
Food Deals 3	$3.00–$6.00 Extensive menu selection of gourmet food and basics too: scallops, ahi, crab cakes, satay, lamb chops, steak Diane, salads, blackened salmon, calamari
Drink Specials 0	No drink specials
Atmosphere 3	Historic and Fancy with a capital “F”, their Lobby Court Bar offers the opportunity to dine in high-style for less. Perfect place to pretend you’re Thurston or Lovey Howell. And its haunted!

7

Old Town

231 SW Ankeny
(503) 248-4579
www.berbati.com

Berbati's Pan

Happy Hours	4:00–7:00pm Daily
Food Deals 2	Yummy $2.00 gyros! Chicken, lamb and vegetarian; hummus and fries specials too.
Drink Specials 3	Only $2.00 for drafts and wells!
Atmosphere 2	Daytime's quiet, pre-nightclub experience is pleasantly peaceful; Greek arches over doors, faux aged walls, funky Aladdin lamps, cool copper studded floor, and art. Outdoor patio (may be self-serve).

"Most folks are about as happy as they make up their minds to be."

– Abraham Lincoln –

7

Alberta

904 NE Alberta
(503) 282-9864
www.berniesbistro.com

Bernie's Southern Bistro

Happy Hours	4:00–6:00pm Tues–Sat 10:00pm–close Tues–Sat
Food Deals 3	$3.00 Gourmet southern samplers including Po' Boys, fried green tomatoes, red beans & rice, salad, sweet potato fries, mac & cheese
Drink Specials 0	No drink specials
Atmosphere 3	Serene outdoor garden patio, and they even let you sit outside for Happy Hour. Quite lovely! Simple, fine-dining, romantic interior.

8

Downtown
(West Map)

1135 SW Washington
(503) 445-8331
www.bettiefordlounge.com

Bettie Ford

Happy Hours	5:00pm–midnight Wed (!) 5:00–9:00pm Thurs & Fri
Food Deals 2	$2.50–$5.00 Veggie stir-fry, onion rings, 1/2 club sandwich w/salad, seasoned, garlic, and regular fries, wings, mozz stix
Drink Specials 3	$2.00 drafts $3.00 wells
Atmosphere 3	Totally different, mellow and blue vibe compared to nighttime nightclub scene; "institutional chic" with funky barred windows and hanging hospital curtains around booths.
Extra Info	Don't miss the hysterically funny, creatively-named cocktail list!

7

Pearl

250 NW 13th Ave.
(503) 226-3394
www.bluehouronline.com

Blue Hour

Happy Hours	4:30–6:30pm Tues–Fri
Food Deals 2	$1.00–$7.00 Limited, but high-end choices: bruschetta plate, pizza, salad, fries, cheese fondue
Drink Specials 2	$3.00 draft beer $4.00 well drinks $5.00 specialty cocktail
Atmosphere 3	Impressive lofted interior; VERY well-designed—a Portland stand-out! Trés trendy and active scene (can be a touch loud); HH sidewalk patio dining allowed.

Belmont Area

3341 SE Belmont
(503) 595-0575
www.thebluemonk.com

Blue Monk

Happy Hours	5:00pm–7:00pm Daily
Food Deals 2	$5.00 "Grub" Nice variety: shrimp tacos, ahi caesar wrap, bruschetta, coconut polenta, meatball & sausage subs, pasta primavera, olive plate
Drink Specials 2	$2.50 wells $3.00 selected beer $4.50 house wine $4.50 specialty cocktails
Atmosphere 2	Mellow & blue low-key jazzy; down tempo vibe with candlelight; cool blue tube lights over bar area.
Extra Info	Impressive selection of Belgian ales (not discounted)—and of course a great jazz club later at night!

7

Hawthorne

3632 SE Hawthorne
(503) 233-6540
www.bridgeportbrewandalehouse.com

Bridgeport Ale House

Happy Hours 3:00–6:00pm Daily

Food Deals 2 $3.00 sandwiches
Grilled portabello, BLT, roasted pork loin, and pulled roasted chicken
Several $8.00 pizzas available too.

Drink Specials 2 $2.50 pints

Atmosphere 2 A smaller neighborhood Bridgeport Brewpub with sleek, contemporary, mission-style stylings; streetside large-scale windows, plus outdoor sidewalk seating during Happy Hour.

7

Pearl

1313 NW Marshall
(503) 241-7179
www.bridgeportbrewandalehouse.com

Bridgeport Brewpub

Happy Hours 4:00–6:00pm Mon–Fri
10:00pm–close Tues–Thurs

Food Deals 2 $2.00–$5.00 (+$10.00 pizzas)
Cheeseburgers, pork sliders, Caesar, spinach artichoke dip, chips & salsa, house-made (bakery) pretzels

Drink Specials 2 $2.75 pints
$4.00 bartender's choice cocktail

Atmosphere 3 Brand-spankin'-new, big-city-style brewery, bakery *and* coffee shop in renovated loft building; cavernous open area with the brick, iron and wood basics; outdoor seating.

5

(Waterfront/ Off the Willamette)

6835 SW Macadam
(503) 244-7111
www.thebuffalogap.com

Buffalo Gap

Happy Hours 4:00–6:00pm
10:00–midnight Mon–Fri

Food Deals 2 $1.95–$3.95
Basic bar standards like brats and tots, fish or chicken tacos, hummus, Caesar, BBQ pork sandwiches

Drink Specials 1 A couple random, domestic pitcher specials mostly revolving around game nights

Atmosphere 2 Reminds me of a typical Midwest small town tourist pub; meandering rooms with some farm-style touches; totally casual place to watch sports.

7

NW/Nob Hill

1639 NW Glisan
(503) 517-8220

Callaloo

Happy Hours 3:00–6:00pm Daily
10:00pm–close Daily

Food Deals 2 $4.50–$9.75
"Island Time" Caribbean plates, unique but pricey for Happy Hour; conch fritters, jerk pork, satay, sweet potato fries, greens

Drink Specials 2 $1.50 PBRs
$2.00 Red Stripe
$4.00 house cocktails

Atmosphere 2 Understated tropical; bar area is simple for an island escape theme but still retains just a touch of mambo mojo.

8

Alberta

2203 NE Alberta
(503) 282-5522

Ciao Vito

Happy Hours	4:00–8:00pm Mon–Wed 4:00–6:00pm Thurs–Sun
Food Deals 2	\$4.00–\$8.00 High quality, but pricier menu items including salads, spaghetti options, burger, veggie sandwich, antipasti
Drink Specials 3	\$2.00 pints \$1.00 off wells \$3.50/\$4.00 wines \$5.00 cocktails
Atmosphere 3	Classic elegance with warmth and style, nice neighborhood welcoming feel with bright and funky mural on outside side wall.
Extra Info	Wednesday night wine pairings

9

Downtown
(East Map)

424 SW 4th Ave.
(503) 221-2489
www.citysportsbar.com

The City

Happy Hours	4:00–7:00pm Mon–Fri (drinks) 4:00–7:00 Daily (food) 10:00–close Daily (food)
Food Deals 2	$1.95–$3.95 14 bar-style standards including wings, nachos, burgers, calamari, cheese fries, lasagna, Caesar salad
Drink Specials 3	$2.00 selected domestic beer $3.00 selected premium pints $3.00 well drinks and cocktails $3.00 drink board with 9 cocktails
Atmosphere 3	Old Chicago-style sports bar; exposed brick & beams; over 30 TVs/2 projection screens! Outdoor sidewalk seating self-serve.
Extra Info	Pint ski beer flights!

8

Lloyd Center-ish

1932 NE Broadway
(503) 288-3333

Colosso

Happy Hours 5:00–7:00pm Daily
5:00–close Sundays

Food Deals 2 $2.00–$4.00
Only 5 choices, but unique and muy delicioso! Avocado salad, squash with zesty tomato, bread garlic chili prawns, salad

Drink Specials 2 $1.00 off draft beer
$1.00 off specialty cocktails

Atmosphere 3 Lush, intimate Spanish decor—you'd half-expect a velvet painting matador to walk in any moment! Metallic gold stucco walls, window arches, red velvet drapes, black wooden tables and cool lamps.

7

North/NE

1329 NE Fremont
(503) 284-4805

County Cork

Happy Hours 4:00–6:00pm Mon–Fri

Food Deals 3 $3.00–$4.00
Good and big meal offerings:
fish & chips, veggie wrap, BLT,
Guiness stew & shepherd's pie with
side salads, turkey wrap, burger

Drink Specials 1 $3.50 most pints
25 notable beers on tap

Atmosphere 2 Big, fun and colorful Irish pub;
a welcoming, friendly shelter.
Hand-painted tables, pub decor,
bench seating, windows that open
to the street, and sidewalk seating.

Extra info Family friendly; live Irish music

6

North/NE

3954 N Mississippi
(503) 280-7099
www.crowbarpdx.com

Crow Bar

Happy Hours	3:00–8:00pm Daily (drinks) 5:00–7:00pm Daily (food)
Food Deals 2	$3.00–$4.00 Limited but unique options; jambalaya, vegan curry, hummus, salmon Caesar salad
Drink Specials 3	$1.50 PBR on tap $2.50 microbrews $2.50 house wines
Atmosphere 1	Dark basic bar with good tunes; trendy—but not pretentious (but smoky and loud).
Extra info	Margarita machine!

7

Belmont Area

1412 SE Morrison
(503) 235-8150
www.crushbar.com

Crush

Happy Hours — All day Tuesdays (food 'til 11:00pm)
4:30–6:00pm Wed–Fri

Food Deals 2 — $3.00–$5.00
13 offerings such as hummus, soup, baba ganoush, variety of breads, flat nachos, BBQ beef sandwich, mushroom skewers (vegan), linguini

Drink Specials 3 — $2.00 Molson's
$3.00 martinis (choice of 4)
$4.00 house red wine
$4.00 Manhattan or classic martini

Atmosphere 2 — Open artsy lounge with stunning bottle chandelier as focal point; a truly comfortable and inviting neighborhood hangout and a big favorite of many loyal locals.

6

Downtown
(West Map)

750 SW Alder St
(503) 294-7001
www.westinportland.com/dailygrill

Daily Grill/Westin

Happy Hours	4:00–7:00pm Mon–Fri
Food Deals 2	$2.95 Mini-cheeseburgers, calamari, spinach artichoke dip, seared ahi, chicken quesadilla, pot pie
Drink Specials 0	No drink specials
Atmosphere 3	Bogart-y '40s-style upscale hotel bar; deep, warm cranberry walls, dark woods and thick moldings; leather booths with cocktail tables.

"Jumping for joy is good exercise."

– Author Unknown –

6

Old Town

208 SW Ankeny St
(503) 227-5906
www.danandlouis.com

Dan & Louis' Oyster Bar

Happy Hours	4:00–6:00pm Mon–Fri
Food Deals 2	$2.95 Cajun pan-fried oysters, clam strips, 1/2 pound cheeseburger, Caesar, onion rings, and $9.95/dozen oysters on the half-shell
Drink Specials 0	No drink discounts
Atmosphere 3	Totally different with small-town, east-coast, casual crabbing charm. Worth ducking in from the alley to this cozy, candlelit, ship-like hideaway.

6

Lloyd Center-ish

830 E Burnside
(503) 231-9663
www.dougfirlounge.com

Doug Fir Lounge

Happy Hours	3:00–6:00pm Daily
Food Deals 2	$2.50 Plentiful portions of comfort food: cheeseburger, biscuits & gravy, ham sandwich (croque monsieur), tomato soup, salad, bread pudding
Drink Specials 1	$3.00 wells
Atmosphere 2	Twin Peaks meets the Sinatra 50's in classy-kitsch Northwest lodge theme; couch pits for groups; outdoor patio seating.
Extra info	Great place to see bands!

10

Downtown (West Map)

909 SW Park Ave.
(503) 243-5991
www.dragonfishcafe.com

Dragonfish

Happy Hours	4:00–6:00pm Daily 10:00pm–close Daily
Food Deals 3	$1.45 nigiri (7 single-piece choices) $1.95 sushi rolls (5 four-piece plates) $1.45–$3.85 small plates including potstickers, lettuce cups, miso soup, ginger chicken, BBQ ribs, edamame
Drink Specials 3	$3.25 drafts $2.75 hot and premium sakes $3.75 bartender's choice creatives
Atmosphere 3	The fun bar side of their restaurant (across the hall) has bamboo, art, a wall of Pachinko game machines, comfy couch seating, and hanging metal art sculptures of sea creatures, with red blinds and shoji screens.

7

Downtown
(West Map)

729 SW 15th Ave.
(503) 223-6311
www.hoteldeluxeportland.com

Driftwood Room

Happy Hours 3:00–6:00pm Daily
9:00pm–close Daily

Food Deals 3 $2.50–$5.00
Half-off plentiful high-end plates: prawn or flank steak bruschetta, mixed greens or Caesar salad, mac & cheese, mussels, crab cakes, spring rolls, burgers/sliders

Drink Specials 0 No drink specials

Atmosphere 3 Off the VERY impressive grand lobby of the Hotel deLuxe, the Driftwood has a dark and discreet ratpack appeal in kidney-shaped, dimly-lit, wooden room with NW touches.

7

Hawthorne

4260 SE Hawthorne
(503) 231-9225
www.theempireroom.net

The Empire Room

Happy Hours	4:00–7:00pm Tues-Sat
Food Deals 2	$5.00 Salami & cheese plate, hummus, artichoke dip, spinach salad, chicken skewers, nachos
Drink Specials 3	$3.00 martinis $3.00 select beer and wine $3.00 well drinks
Atmosphere 2	Very charming and delightful old Victorian with hand-painted vines on walls; cute raised window seats, and a sweet & serene feel.

"Scatter sunshine."

– Norman Vincent Peale –

7

Downtown
(East Map)

824 SW First Ave.
(503) 248-4709
www.fernandosportland.com

Fernando's Hideaway

Happy Hours	4:30–close Mondays 4:30–7:00pm Tues-Sun
Food Deals 1	Excellent food, but Happy Hour food specials limited to Mondays only (2-for-1 tapas); Otherwise, 24 delicious unique tapas under $4.00 at all times
Drink Specials 3	$3.00 house wine $2.50 microbrews Doubles on most cocktails
Atmosphere 3	High-beamed, artsy, lofted, brick; Spanish-style loaded with charm and personalidad.
Extra Info	Free salsa lessons Thursday, Friday, and Saturday at 9:00pm

306 NW Broadway
(503) 222-4458
www.giltclub.com

Gilt Club

Happy Hours 5:00–6:30pm Mon–Fri

Food Deals 3 $1.00–$7.00
11 Delicious upscale offerings: biscotti, olives, fries, ribs, Caesar and Caprese salads, mussels, grilled shrimp, bruschetta, burgers

Drink Specials 2 $2.50 Stellas
$5.00 wine
$5.00 most excellent cocktails

Atmosphere 3 Yes, it IS most luscious! Plushness abounds with deep red walls and velvet drapes with gold touches & sexy curves galore. WAY swanky!

7

Pearl

939 NW 10th Ave.
(503) 808-9888
www.grazerestaurant.com

Graze

Happy Hours	4:00–7:00pm Mon–Sat
Food Deals 2	$4.00 Several small plate delights that that change with seasonal freshness: Caesar, polenta cake, fries, tasty fried calamari, eggplant rolls
Drink Specials 2	$3.00 select pints $6.00–$7.00 wine specials
Atmosphere 2	Inside a building of windows; ultra sleek and minimalist; creamy faux aged backdrops with candles and modern black trim and tables.

7

Downtown (East Map)

404 SW Washington
(503) 224-2288
www.greekcusina.com

Greek Cusina

Happy Hours	3:00–6:00pm Mon–Fri
Food Deals 3	$2.75–$5.50 (1/2 off—oopa!) Garlic shrimp, pesto chicken, grilled veggies, pitas, calamari, salmon cakes, zucchini parmesan
Drink Specials 2	$3.00 drafts $3.00 wells
Atmosphere 2	Outside marked by landmark giant purple octopus; Mediterranean decor & color scheme; booths with big open windows/walls; very fun octopus lamps.

7

Downtown (West Map)

1135 SW Morrison
(503) 248-2112

Green Papaya

Happy Hours 4:00–6:00pm Daily (food only)
9:00pm–12:00am Thurs–Sat
(drinks discounted too)

Food Deals 3 Nicely presented selection of Vietnamese goodies (20 items): satay, coconut prawns, sesame steak rolls, wontons, spring rolls, potstickers, tofu skewers, salads

Drink Specials 1 (Offered late-night hours only)
$3.00 wells
$1.00 off house drinks

Atmosphere 2 Downplayed/basic with some nice Asian-style touches; ceilings covered in giant white paper lanterns.

Extra Info Restaurant entrance opens later (enter bar side off 12th Ave.)

7

Downtown
(East Map)

204 SW Yamhill
(503) 241-8132

H2O

Happy Hours	4:00–8:00pm Tues–Sun
Food Deals 3	$1.75–$5.00 Shrimp tempura, crispy ahi sticks, crepes, Angus cheeseburger, hot & cold sandwiches, wings, soup, garlic fries, hummus, salads,
Drink Specials 1	$5.00 cosmos & lemon drops
Atmosphere 2	Entirely midnight black interior with wave-shaped silver details. Gorgeous mermaid water fountain art piece at nightclub entrance.

7★

Downtown
(West Map)

1001 SW Broadway
(503) 241-4100
www.heathmanhotel.com

The Heathman Hotel

Happy Hours	4:00–6:00pm Daily 9:00pm–close Daily All day on Thursdays!
Food Deals 3	$2.25–$5.00 Lots of unique gourmet samplings: seared ahi, oysters, mussels, paté, crab cake, salads, dips, burger, cheese plate, soups
Drink Specials 0	No drink specials
Atmosphere 3	Two traditional upscale rooms: the quiet romantic Tea Court in back with giant marble fireplace, and the well-stocked Marble Bar, very popular with the after work crowd.
Extra Info	A Portland landmark since 1927

7★

Pearl

10 NW 12th Ave.
(503) 227-5320
www.henrystavern.com

Henry's Tavern

Happy Hours	3:00–6:00pm Daily 9:00–close Sun–Wed 10:30pm–close Thurs–Sat
Food Deals 3	1.95–$3.95 Gorgonzola fries(!!!), cheeseburger, steak sandwich, satay, sushi rolls, BBQ chicken pizza, wings, soup, avocado & mango salad, crabcakes
Drink Specials 0	No drink specials
Atmosphere 3	A long-time Portland favorite; FUN spacious transformed ex-brewery; open two-story seating; huge center bar; loft-style bricks & iron; patio (not available for HH seating).
Extra Info	Over 100 beers on tap!

7

Downtown
(East Map)

411 SW 3rd Ave.
(503) 228-5686
www.hubers.com

Huber's

Happy Hours 4:30–6:30pm Daily
9:30pm–close Daily

Food Deals 3 $1.95–$3.95
Wide variety of appetizers with a good mix of options: turkey sandwich, enchiladas, quesadillas, tuna, fried calamari, burgers, salad

Drink Specials 0 No drink specials

Atmosphere 3 Historic architecture and design; giant domed stained-glass ceiling; open tables and cozy booths make it a pleasant warm meeting place. Watch the Spanish coffee "shows"!

Extra Info Portland's oldest restaurant

8

Hawthorne

2229 SE Hawthorne
(503) 239-4002
www.takeitin.com

Imbibe

Happy Hours
4:00–7:000pm Daily
11:00–12:00pm Sun–Thur

Food Deals 3
$4.50
Six full-meal sized offerings:
best burger (Painted Hills) in the city!
Also veggie sandwich, wings,
Caesar, mac & cheese

Drink Specials 2
$.75 off beer ($3.00 average)
$3.00 well drinks

Atmosphere 3
Metropolitan swanky chic decor;
wall-size windows open to outside;
good (but very loud) live music.

7

Downtown
(West Map)

401 SW 12th Ave.
(503) 226-1419
www.jakesfamouscrawfish.com

Jake's Famous Crawfish

Happy Hours	3:00–6:00pm Mon–Fri 10:00–close Sun–Thurs 11:00pm–close Fri–Sat
Food Deals 3	$1.95–$3.95 Some outstanding hearty sizes! Cheeseburger or chicken sandwich WITH fries only $1.95(!), fish & chips, seafood tacos, calamari, hummus, pot stickers, seared ahi tuna
Drink Specials 0	No drink specials
Atmosphere 3	A Portland landmark since 1892; old-school fun with traditional class; outdoor sidewalk dining.

7 ★

Downtown
(West Map)

611 SW Tenth Ave.
(503) 220-1850
www.jakesgrill.com

Jake's Grill

Happy Hours

3:00–6:00pm Mon–Fri
9:30–close Mon–Thurs
10:00pm–close Fri–Sat
3:00pm–close Sundays

Food Deals 3

$1.95 all menu items
Similar to the other Jake's menu with outstanding hearty sizes: wings, cheeseburger or chicken sandwich with fries, prawn skewers, hummus, bruschetta, pot stickers, mussels

Drink Specials 0

No drink specials

Atmosphere 3

Stately & traditional with convivial class; fancy white jacket and bowtie servers; connected with impressive Governor Hotel.

6

Downtown
(East Map)

826 SW 2nd Ave.
(503) 228-9128
www.jaxbar.com

Jax

Happy Hours	3:00–6:00pm Mon–Fri 10:00pm–midnight Mon–Sat 11am–11pm Sunday!
Food Deals 2	$2.75–$3.75 Prawn & artichoke dip, nachos, quesadillas, wings, hummus plate, Caesar, burger, pizza
Drink Specials 2	$3.25 micros $3.25 wells $2.75 import bottles $2.00 domestic beer
Atmosphere 2	Clean & simple garage-style room open to outside and sidewalk, black overhead girders, and overhead TVs.
Extra Info	Rooftop deck with view of Mt. Hood

7

NW/Nob Hill

715 NW 23rd Ave.
(503) 222-0048
www.papahaydn.com/r/6/Jo-Bar

Jo-Bar

Happy Hours	3:00–6:00pm Daily
Food Deals 2	$3.00–$7.00 Asian veggie ravioli, French onion soup, crab cakes, pizza, salads
Drink Specials 2	$5.00 exceptional cocktails
Atmosphere 2	Deep red and olive walls, stunning entry flower display, original art, huge iron chandelier, open stone rotisserie oven, full front windows, outdoor sidewalk seating.

"A hangover is the wrath of grapes."

– Author Unknown –

7

Old Town

112 SW Second Ave.
503 227 4057
www.kellsirish.com/portland

Kell's Irish Pub

Happy Hours 4:00–7:00pm Mon–Fri
10:00pm–midnight Mon–Thurs
7:00–10:00pm Sunday

Food Deals 3 $3.00
Irish nachos, wings, Caesar, BLT, burger or sandwich with fries, quesadilla, oyster shooters, chicken curry & chips, Gorgonzola spread

Drink Specials 0 No drink specials

Atmosphere 3 Gorgeous ornate ceiling—no, wait—those are wrinkled dollar bills... You KNOW a good time is to be had in this infamous Portland Institution! It's just F-U-N!

Extra Info Meeting and party/reception rooms

10

Belmont Area

2304 SE Belmont
(503) 239-9675

La Calaca Comelona

Happy Hours	8:00pm–close Mon–Sat
Food Deals 3	$1.00–$6.00 Finalmente! True delicious Mexican food in Portland: pork & pineapple tacos (plus other varieties); grilled cactus, spicy potatoes, quesadillas, taquitos—and grilled grasshoppers!
Drink Specials 3	Rotating menu of all kinds of drink discounts off all kinds of drinks
Atmosphere 3	Take a Mexican vacation to this Day-of-the Dead-inspired taverna named "The Hungry Skeleton." Bright colorful walls, Mexican-style folk art at every glimpse and turn, plus a delightful beer garden!

6

NW/Nob Hill

2327 NW Kearney
(503) 228-5553
www.laurelwoodbrewpub.com

Laurelwood / NW

Happy Hours	3:00–6:00pm Daily 9:00–11:00pm Daily
Food Deals 2	$3.95 BBQ pork quesadillas, burgers, happy nachos, chili/cheese and garlic fries, buffalo chicken strips
Drink Specials 1	$1 off pints ($2.75)
Atmosphere 2	Cozy restaurant in big old victorian; converted rooms feel like home; outdoor seating on two porches; upstairs has some loud family fun....
Extra Info	Organic beer Other Location: 1728 NE 40th (503) 335-9084

Pearl

300 NW 10th Ave.
(503) 224-1680

Life of Riley

Happy Hours	4:00–7:00pm Daily
Food Deals 2	$2.50–$4:00 Buffalo chili, buffalo wings, fries, kettle chips, calamari, piglets in blanket, roasted mussels
Drink Specials 2	$3.00 drafts (many great choices!)
Atmosphere 2	The old Jimmy Mak's with a bit nicer look; an open navy room; casual, retro, semi-Irish decor; rare ultra-casual option in the Pearl.

3901 N. Williams
(503) 288-3996
www.newoldlompoc.com/5qhome

Lompoc Fifth Quadrant

Happy Hours	4:00–6:00pm Mon-Fri 11:00am–close Sat & Sun
Food Deals 2	$3.00 Cheaper versions of their regular appetizer dishes: great hummus plate, artichoke hearts, nachos, clams, fries, meat & cheese platter
Drink Specials 2	$2.00 pints all day Tuesdays $2.75 beers other Happy Hours $2.00 Bloody Mary Sundays (spicy!)
Atmosphere 2	Brand new, colorful, loft-style brewpub; big long wooden booths for socializing; outdoor patio open to restaurant—and open to Happy Hour revelers as well!

NW/Nob Hill

704 NW 21st Ave.
(503) 226-6126
www.lucystable.com

Lucy's Table

Happy Hours 5:00–6:30pm Mon–Fri

Food Deals 3 $2.00–$4.50
Half-off delicious bar menu!
Goat cheese ravioli, pastas, ribs, beef brochettes, burgers, prawns, salads, mussels, oysters

Drink Specials 3 $2.75 draft beer
$3.25 well drinks
$3.50 select red & white wine
$4.00 select cocktails

Atmosphere 3 A kind of tight bar area with a kind of Pottery Barn-ish simplicity. Very nice and appealing space where you'll be focusing on the great food more than anything!

6

(Waterfront/ Off the Willamette)

5833 SW Macadam
(503) 246-6227
www.macadamsbarandgrill.com

Macadams

Happy Hours	3:00–6:00pm Daily 10:00pm–close Sun–Thurs
Food Deals 2	$2.95–$4.95 Basic bar items including cheese fries, fried calamari, Buffalo wings, mac & cheese, Caesar, burgers, quesadillas, pork sandwiches
Drink Specials 2	$.50 cents off drafts $4.00 house wines $4.00 or $5.00 cocktail of the night
Atmosphere 2	Upscale, lofted lodge effect with traditional manly-man tans and browns. Plenty of TVs for watching your favorite games. Outdoor area.

Belmont area

1109 SE Madison
(503) 230-2471
www.meet-at-madisons.com

Madison's

Happy Hours 3:00–6:00pm Daily
10:00pm–close Daily (food & drink)

Food Deals 3 $1.95–$4.50
Half-off all appetizers (good sized): crab cakes, quesadillas, tabasco buffalo wings, nachos, hummus, onion rings, salads, artichoke dip

Drink Specials 3 $1.75 domestic drafts
$3.00 microbrews
$3.50 well drinks
$3.50 select wines

Atmosphere 2 Friendly, casual hang-out place; nice, but seen-it-before-decor; outdoor wood deck available for Happy Hour patrons.

7

Downtown
(East Map)

439 SW 2nd Ave.
(503) 295-6464
www.mamamiatrattoria.com

Mama Mia's

Happy Hours	5:00–7:00pm Mon–Fri 11:00am–midnight Fri&Sat
Food Deals 3	$3.00 Plentiful and delicious pasta dishes including meatballs, pasta dishes, pasta-free lasagna, manicotti, Caesar salad, minestrone, plus fried calamari and zucchini
Drink Specials 0	No drink specials
Atmosphere 3	Mama mia! Now that's Italian! Dripping in old world ambience with nearly 100 gilded mirrors, 20 chandeliers, red velvet, gold gilding, red-checks everywhere, PLUS romantic candlelight.

7★

Pearl

1203 NW Glisan
(503) 248-1690
www.manzanagrill.com

Manzana's

Happy Hours 4:00–6:00pm Mon–Fri
11:00am–close Tues, Sat & Sun

Food Deals 3 $1.95–$3.95
Chipotle barbecue pork quesadilla, citrus honey chicken wings, BBQ sandwich, Southwestern salad, hummus, crab cakes, chicken wrap

Drink Specials 0 No drink specials

Atmosphere 3 Mmmm... the rotisserie smell! Deep, dark, rich wooden booths and walls (new and modern), low lighting, outdoor sidewalk dining during Happy Hour.

Other location:
305 1st Street
(503) 675-3322
On the lake, but inside HH seating.

9

Downtown (West Map)

406 SW 13th Ave
(503) 221-6278
www.masusushi.com

Masu

Happy Hours 4:30–6:00pm Daily
10:00–close Sun–Thurs
11:00pm–close Fri & Sat

Food Deals 2 $2.00–$5.00
I went in not liking sushi and came out loving it! Delicious, but limited choices of daily nigiri and rolls, soba salad, miso cod, veggie maki, yum yum stix, edamame

Drink Specials 3 $3.00 tap beer
$3.50 wells
$5.00 list of specialty cocktails

Atmosphere 3 Unique "retro-Asian" lounge; open and boxy with Jenga-style wood blocks covering the walls and back bar; stunning, colorful hand-painted mural.

7★

Waterfront

0309 SW Montgomery
(503) 220-1865
www.mccormickandschmicks.com

McCormick & Schmick's

Happy Hours 4:00–6:00pm Daily
9:00pm–close Daily
Hours vary slightly per location

Food Deals 3 $1.95–3.95
Delicious menu is just a bit different at each restaurant. All are GREAT!

Drink Specials 0 No drink specials

Atmosphere 3 Classic places you could take mom.

Other Locations:
235 SW 1st Ave.—Portland
(503) 224-7522

Bridgeport Village—Tigard
17015 SW 72nd Ave.
(503) 684-5490

9945 SW Beaverton-Hillsdale Hwy.
—Beaverton
(503) 643-1322

6

Old Town

107 NW Couch
(503) 220-5055
www.mcfaddensportland.com

McFadden's

Happy Hours	4:00–7:00pm Mon–Fri
Food Deals 2	$3.00 and $4.00 Bar-style old-world comfort food; burger and pork sliders, penne, bangers, Guiness beef stew, mac & cheese, Caesar, soup
Drink Specials 1	$1 off Miller beers
Atmosphere 2	Brand new look of old Irish Pub; BIG wooden bars with brick walls; huge party space with dance floor and 50+ TVs!
Extra Info	Good for groups and parties

They're everywhere!

Hotels, movies, live bands, pubs
www.mcmenamins.com

McMenamins

Giant kudos & cheers!

Okay, so I'm breaking out of the box a bit now to give this group of restuarants special focus. I am a HUGE fan of the McMenamins establishments! I especially love their hotel properties which are some truly special, not-to-be-missed Portland experiences. They really know how to pull together unique spaces loaded with personality (and maybe ghosts)! There's always lots to look at and they pick up on some very interesting and creative themes. Happy-Hour-wise, they're only average according to my established guidelines, but they are surely most excellent places! Their menu has lots of cheap eats, so just go at any time. Most places have small discounts on food and beer 4:00–6:00pm Mon–Fri. Also note that you can drink beer and eat inside their movie theaters! Although this is a Portland city-focused book, for reference purposes, I've included info on some of their stellar places outside of Portland city limits.

Hotel and bar listings on the following pages...

McMenamins Hotels

Edgefield
2126 SW Halsey
Troutdale, OR
(503) 669-8610
38-acre renovated "Poor Farm"; golf, movies, beer garden, fine-dining, wine bar, Jerry Garcia bar, Little Red Shed Pub, Power Station restaurant

The Grand Lodge
3505 Pacific Ave.
Forest Grove, OR
(503) 992-9533
Stately but fun ex-Masonic and nursing home; multiple restaurants; cozy, small bars, movies, soaking tub

Hotel Oregon
310 NE Evans Street
McMinnville, OR
(503) 472-8427
Weekend get-away in wine country; rooftop bar (great for viewing UFOs), pub, back bar, Cellar Bar, pool/billiards

Kennedy School
5736 NE 33rd Ave.
Portland, OR
(503) 249-3983
Detention Bar, Honors Bar, movies, soaking pool, outdoor courtyard beer garden, party/meeting rooms, restaurant

Old St. Francis School
700 NW Bond Street
Bend, OR
(541) 382-5174
An old 1936 Catholic schoolhouse transformed into another heavenly entertainment complex

White Eagle
836 N. Russell
Portland, OR
(503) 335-8900
A small "rock 'n' roll hotel" with resident "spirits," nightly bands, a saloon, and outdoor seasonal beer garden

McMenamins Bars

(Select Portland-Area Taverns)

Bagdad Theater
3702 SE Hawthorne
Old Hollywood glamour in Arabian Nights inspired movie theater and restaurant; outdoor sidewalk seating

Blue Moon Tavern
432 NW 21st Ave.
(503) 223-3184
Meandering bar with table-top fireplace in the round and pool tables; outdoor sidewalk seating

Crystal Ballroom
1332 W. Burnside
(503) 225-0047
Awesome place to see bands! The ballroom floor "floats" and there's '80s nights at Lola's.

McMenamins on Broadway
1504 NE Broadway
(503) 288-9498
Great pre-positioning for shopping, Blazers game or a movie

McMenamins on the Columbia
1801 SE Columbia River Dr.
Vancouver, WA
(360) 699-1521
Beautiful view of the Columbia; imbibe along their river side strip

McMenamins Tavern & Pool
1716 NW 23rd Ave.
(503) 227-0929
Heated outdoor tables; pool

Mission
1624 NW Glisan
(503) 223-4527
$3.00 movies in old Swedish Evangelical Mission

Ram's Head
2282 NW Hoyt
(503) 221-0098
Sophisticated manly-man haven

Ringler's Pub
1332 W. Burnside
(503) 225-0627
Funky Ex-auto garage

212 SW Stark
(503) 464-1122
www.mothersbistro.com

Mother's

Happy Hours 3:00–6:00pm Tues–Sat

Food Deals 2 $3.00
Fried ravioli, chicken quesadilla, mini-burger, deviled eggs, hummus, chopped liver & teenie weenies :)

Drink Specials 3 $2.95 tap beer
$3.00 wells
$5.00 array of infused cocktails

Atmosphere 2 Like being welcomed into your rich, Southern grandmother's home with ornate gilded mirrors, chandeliers, and flocked wallpaper everywhere.

"Beer is proof that God loves us and wants us to be happy."

– Benjamin Franklin –

8

NW/Nob Hill

612 NW 21st Ave.
(503) 223-8169

Muu-Muu's

Happy Hours 3:00–6:00pm Mon–Fri

Food Deals 2 $2.00 and $3.00
Most excellent spicy wings, also beef and chicken satay, Brutus (a.k.a. Caesar) salad, Caprese salad, fried calamari, hummus plate

Drink Specials 3 $1.50 PBRs
$2.50 wells & microbrews
$3.50 martinis

Atmosphere 2 Subtle, artsy decor from the top on down; black iron ceiling tiles, orange hanging lights; velvet drapes, giant urn lamps, tiny bubble lights.

6

NW/Nob Hill

1616 NW 23rd Ave.
(503) 225-1855
www.newoldlompoc.com

New Old Lompoc

Happy Hours	4:00–7:00pm Daily Drink specials all day Sat & Sun
Food Deals 2	$2.95 Pork sandwich w/fries, hummus, artichoke hearts, sausage, fries
Drink Specials 1	$2.75 pints
Atmosphere 2	Heavenly-hops-covered back patio is the biggest draw here. Laid-back casual scene with picnic tables inside.
Extra Info	Miser Mondays with $2.00 drafts Bloody Marys $2.00 all day Sunday

8

Waterfront
(Jantzen Beach)

11950 N Center Ave.
(503) 283-3474
www.newportbay.com

Newport Bay

Happy Hours 3:00–7:00pm Daily
9:00pm–close Daily

Food Deals 3 $1.99–$3.99
Fish tacos, pear & pecan salad, clam chowder, fish & chips, onion rings, shrimp cocktail, crab cakes, prawn skewers, halibut sandwich

Drink Specials 2 $1.00 off pints
$1.00 off well drinks

Atmosphere 2 Cape Cod boater casual with city style; white wood walls with indoor windows; copper-topped tables around small traditional bar.

Other Portland Location:
Newport Riverplace/Marina
0425 SW Montgomery
(503) 227-3474
(menu may vary, no drink specials)

7

Lloyd Center-area

1200 NE Broadway
(503) 493-0100
www.newportseafoodgrill.com

Newport Seafood Grill

Happy Hours 3:00–6:00pm Daily

Food Deals 3 $1.95–$3.95
15 varied menu items including clam chowder, fish & chips, salads, sushi rolls, crab cakes, fish tacos

Drink Specials 0 No drink specials

Atmosphere 3 Owned by those bar gods at Pacific Coast Restaurant Family. Popular big bustling bar area, upscale casual, clean simple decor.

Extra Info Conveniently located near the movie theaters at Lloyd Center

Belmont Area

2100 SE Clinton
(503) 731-6500
www.nightlightlounge.net

Night Light Lounge

Happy Hours	3:00–7:00pm Daily
Food Deals 3	$2.00–$5.00 13 items: unique quesadillas, several salads, baguettes, soup, big plates of nachos ($2.00!)
Drink Specials 2	$1.00 off well drinks and wine $1.50 PBRs $3.00 microbrews (a few cheaper wine options and $3.00 bottled beer at all times)
Atmosphere 2	Artsy and upscale with casual, comfortable, yet trendy feel; outdoor dining both on back deck and front sidewalk.

Pearl

10

555 NW 12th Ave.
(503) 228-6161
www.obarestaurant.com

Oba!

Happy Hours 4:00–6:30pm Mon–Sat
9:30pm–close Mon–Thurs (food only)
4:00pm–close Sundays

Food Deals 3 $3.50–$6.00
12 muy delicioso items: grilled salmon tostada, jerked fries with spicy aioli, coconut prawns, tacos, salad, spiced pita chips

Drink Specials 3 $3.75 fresh fruit Margaritas
$3.75 selected draft beer
$3.50 house wine

Atmosphere 3 Colorful, fun and trendy scene; outdoor sidewalk dining.

1338 NW Hoyt
(503) 274-0800
www.olearestaurant.com

Olea

Happy Hours 5:00–7:00pm Mon–Fri

Food Deals 3 $2.00–$5.00
Excellent and unusual samplings (head chef hails from the French Laundry): grilled dates, crispy brie, cheese and sausage selections, pizza, spanakopita, hummus

Drink Specials 0 No drink specials

Atmosphere 3 Huge warehouse-sized dining room with soaring ceilings and windows; upscale & impressive industrial styling; outdoor sidewalk dining.

9

Pearl

910 NW 14th Ave.
(503) 227-7020
www.ondecksportsbar.com

On Deck Sports

Happy Hours	3:30–7:00pm Mon–Fri 9:00pm–close Mon–Fri
Food Deals 3	$1.95–$4.50 Bar food taken up a notch in quality and quantity: bratwurst, 1/2 lb. burgers or BBQ pork sliders including fries, wings, pizza, Caesar, potato skins, pretzels, fries
Drink Specials 2	Changes nightly, but goes 'til close!
Atmosphere 3	Really as nice as a sports bar can be: half red-brick-colored walls / half wall-to-wall windows; wavy black ceiling tiles; hi-def TVs surrounding the rounded bar in middle.

6

Downtown (East Map)

65 SW Yamhill
(503) 224-5626
www.paddys.com

Paddy's

Happy Hours
3:00–6:00pm Mon–Fri
10:00–close Mon–Fri
All day Sunday

Food Deals 2
$3.75
Mini phyllo wraps, nachos, tempura corn dog, skins, wings, onion rings, jalapeno poppers, chicken fingers

Drink Specials 1
$3.75 NW microbrew drafts
$3.75 wells

Atmosphere 2
Warm, upscale Irish pub with a gianormous wooden bar stacked sky-high with spirits of all sorts; outdoor sidewalk seating.

5

Old Town

105 NW 3rd Ave.
(503) 242-0700
www.palalounge.com

Pala Fashion Lounge

Happy Hours	7:00–9:00pm Tues–Sat 7:00–close Sundays
Food Deals 2	$2.95 Mini-burgers, pork or sausage sandwiches on a roll, calamari, tots, fries, battered zucchini, mushrooms, and calamari, pizza, ravioli, potstickers
Drink Specials 0	No drink specials
Atmosphere 2	For a nightclub with a supposed fashion flair, it's pretty stark. More underground brick tunnel than anything like runway chic. Good for grabbing a later Happy Hour, or to go early for a table, but best later at night.

Lloyd Center-ish

2811 NE Glisan
(503) 233-0511
www.pambiche.com

Pambiche

Happy Hours	2:00–6:00pm Mon–Fri 10:00pm–midnight Fri & Sat
Food Deals 3	$2.75 all items Mmmmpenadas, fried plantains, salads, rice dishes, fried chicken and pork, shredded beef, stew, and don't miss the desserts!
Drink Specials 2	$2.75 Peruvian Cristal beer $2.75 house red and white wines $4.00 Sangrias (try the white!!)
Atmosphere 3	La Hora del Amigo at a fun and colorful Cuban café; outdoor dining area streetside, bright and happy inside; vibrant exterior!

2401 NE Fremont
(503) 287-3655
www.perrysonfremont.com

Perry's

Happy Hours 4:00–6:00pm Tues–Sat

Food Deals 2 $3.50 all items
Sesame Thai chicken, nachos, veggie enchilada, salads, sauteed polenta, spaghetti, tacos

Drink Specials 0 No drink specials

Atmosphere 3 Like a traveler/artist's home; impressive iron work greeting, masks, decorated atrium sky lights, paintings, ethnic and art statues.

"Enjoy the little things, for one day you may look back and realize they were big things."

– Robert Brault –

7 ★

Downtown
(East Map)

121 SW Third Ave.
(503) 223-6200
www.portlandchophouse.com

Portland Steak & Chophouse

Happy Hours 3:30–6:30pm Mon–Sat
9:30pm–close Mon–Sat
All day Sundays (noon–close)

Food Deals 3 $1.95–$3.95
Upscale menu including steak skewers, 1/4 lb. grilled cheeseburger, salads, crab cakes, spring rolls

Drink Specials 0 No drink specials

Atmosphere 3 Located in Embassy Suites; fancy steak restaurant dining on the cheap; rich wood and private booths; white tablecloths.

7

Downtown
(East Map)

111 SW Fifth Ave., 30th Floor
(503) 450-0030
www.portlandcitygrill.com

Portland City Grill

Happy Hours	4:30–6:30pm Mon–Sat 10:00pm–midnight Mon–Thurs 4:00pm–close Sunday
Food Deals 3	$1.95–$3.95 About 18 outstanding menu items: fresh salads, burgers, spring rolls, pork sandwiches, crab cakes, ahi
Drink Specials 0	No drink specials
Atmosphere 3	WAY higher than just a "3" for atmosphere on a clear day! Portland's highest building hosts one of our best Happy Hours; Perfect for out-of-town guests!
Extra Info	Free parking at Unico US Bancorp Tower (2-1/2 hour max.) Get there before it opens and wait in line if you want a window table!

6

Downtown
(West Map)

830 SW 6th Ave.
(503) 944-1090
www.portoterra.com

Porto Terra

Happy Hours	3:30–7:00pm Mon–Fri
Food Deals 2	$2.50–$4.50 $6.50–$7.50 pizzas Tuscan appetizers: antipastos, ciabatta, bruschetta, calamari, clam steamers, salad
Drink Specials 0	No drink specials
Atmosphere 3	Hilton hotel bar with Tuscan countryside modern motif; a low-key slice of Italy.

7

Lloyd Center-ish

2755 NE Broadway
(503) 288-7687

Pour

Happy Hours	4:30–6:30pm Daily
Food Deals 1	$2.00 Very good, but only options are cheese panini, marinated olives, and roasted hazelnuts
Drink Specials 2	$3.00 pours of select red and white wines of the night $5.00 off select bottles $2.00 Stellas
Atmosphere 3	Striking 1960's-style Space Odyssey lounge; cool white retro chairs and walls; string art mural; silver and real flower touches.

10

Waterfront

320 Oswego Pointe Dr.
(503) 697-8818
www.theram.com/or-lakeoswego.php

RAM Brewery

Happy Hours 3:00–6:00pm Daily
9:00pm–close Sun–Thur
10:00pm–close Fri & Sat

Food Deals 3 $2.00–$5.00
Many, many half-priced goodies: coconut shrimp, burgers, wings, lettuce wraps, dips, nachos, BBQ quesadilla, artichoke dip

Drink Specials 3 $2.50 house wines, well drinks and Big Horn Brewery pints; PLUS daily rotating specials

Atmosphere 3 Ahhh... I absolutely LOVE it here on a warm sunny day! Riverfront outdoor deck (seasonal); sports bar / lake lodge look; lots of TVs of all sizes, and pool tables.

6

Downtown
(East Map)

503 SW Alder
(503) 222-0005
www.redstartavern.com

Red Star Tavern

Happy Hours	4:00–6:00pm Daily 10:00pm–midnight Daily 3:00pm–11:00pm Sundays
Food Deals 2	$3.00 Southern pecan-crusted chicken, pizza, wings, sliders, fritters, Andouille sausage, Caesar salad
Drink Specials 0	No drink specials
Atmosphere 3	Romantic and upscale classy with small nod to rustic charm; see-through walls to interesting street-scapes; big booth options for some serious lounging; plus a nice long bar.

6

Downtown (East Map)

529 SW 4th Ave.
(503) 228-7605
www.rialtopoolroom.com

Rialto

Happy Hours 4:00–7:00pm Mon–Fri

Food Deals 2 $2.00–$4.75
Burgers with fries, Buffalo wings, potato melt, pizzas, coconut shrimp

Drink Specials 2 $1.00 off microbrews
$1.00 off wells

Atmosphere 2 Large, open, and bright pool room with tables in good condition; casual in tone; also has snooker, off-track betting, and pinball.

"When I read about the evils of drinking, I gave up reading."

– Henry Youngman –

7★

NW/Nob Hill

2165 NW Burnside
(503) 223-1513
www.ringsidesteakhouse.com

Ringside

Happy Hours	9:45pm–close Daily 4:00–6:00 pm Sundays
Food Deals 3	$2.25 each Steak bites (YUM!), fish bites, wings, prime rib, ground steak burger, chili poppers, garlic bread, Caesars, fried oysters & shooters
Drink Specials 0	No drink specials
Atmosphere 3	WOW! Now THIS is "old-school"! Fiery, 40's-style, atmospheric, wrap-around patron bar with bartender pit showcasing flaming Spanish coffee-making artistry.

10

Waterfront

470 SW Hamilton Ct.
(503) 802-5850
www.riversatavalonhotel.com

Rivers

Happy Hours	3:30–6:00pm Mon–Sat 3:30–close Sundays
Food Deals 3	\$2.50–\$7.00 (1/2 off) Salads, satays, salmon tartar; burger w/fries, mussels, clams; blue cheese fries; crab cakes; Alaskan king crab legs (1 lb.) \$12.00!
Drink Specials 3	4-for-\$4.00 adorable mini-martinis! \$3.00 selected draught beers \$4.00 red or white wines
Atmosphere 3	Like sitting inside a funky martini: super fun olive bar stools, swirling jewel-toned patterns, glowing color-tiled bar, lounge couches and HUGE window views of the river.
Extra Info	FREE valet parking

6

Downtown
(East Map)

206 SW Morrison
(503) 796-2739
www.rockbottom.com

Rock Bottom

Happy Hours

3:00–6:00pm Mon–Fri
9:00pm–close Sun–Thurs
11:00pm–close Fri & Sat

Food Deals 2

$1.95–$4.95
11 tasty bar basics: sliders, wings, mac & cheese, calamari, nachos, enchiladas, Caesar salad, ahi tuna

Drink Specials 0

No drink specials

Atmosphere 3

Corporate-style open brewery; Warm coppers mixed with wood under soaring lofted ceilings; bustling big bar area; sidewalk dining.

6

Belmont Area

532 SE Grand Ave.
(503) 238-6996
www.roseandraindrop.com

Rose & Raindrop

Happy Hours	4:00–6:00pm Mon–Fri 10:00pm–midnight Mon–Fri
Food Deals 2	$2.00–$4.00 Mostly New Orleans food items: mac & cheese, salad, catfish, soup, hummus, crawfish cakes (yum!)
Drink Specials 0	No drink specials
Atmosphere 3	Gorgeous step back in time; ex-Vaudevillian theatre and old nickelodeon; loads of charm.

1700 N Killingsworth
(503) 285-1200
www.rouxrestaurant.us

Roux

Happy Hours	4:30–6:00pm Daily
Food Deals 2	$4.00–$10.00 ($2 off regular prices) Extra delicious, but expensive food: salads, soup, oysters, catfish. Get the stellar crawfish pie!
Drink Specials 0	No drink specials
Atmosphere 3	Fine dining with simple styling; old elevator shaft remains; nice dinner booths and music.
Extra Info	Wonderful regular dinner place; Located WEST of Hwy. 5

7

North/NE

2731 N Killingsworth
(503) 247-0500
www.salskitchen.com

Sal's Famous Italian

Happy Hours 4:00–6:00pm Daily

Food Deals 2 $2.50–$5.00
Delicious steamed mussels plus calamari, pizza, ravioli, and burgers

Drink Specials 2 $2.50 selected beer
$1.00 off well drinks
$5.00 featured cocktails

Atmosphere 2 Hip AND quaint old-world Italian; outdoor sidewalk seating.

Extra Info Located WEST of Hwy. 5

Other Location:
33 NW 23rd Pl.
(503) 467-4067

10

Waterfront

3839 NE Marine Drive
(503) 288-4444
www.saltys.com

Salty's

Happy Hours	3:00–6:00pm Mon–Sat
Food Deals 3	$1.95–$4.99 Blackened salmon Caesar, prawns, fish & chips, seafood chowder, ravioli, burgers, artichoke dip
Drink Specials 3	$3.25 microbrews $4.25 Margaritas & Bloody Marys $5.00 wine selections
Atmosphere 3	Fine-dining waterside restaurant; wall-to-wall giant windows and outdoor deck; yacht club motif.
Extra Info	GORGEOUS scenery along the river; great place to watch the sunset; views of river and Mt. Hood; free live jazz after 7:00pm Fri & Sat

9

Belmont Area

2236 SE Belmont
(503) 234-0896
www.salvadormollys.com

Salvador Molly's

Happy Hours	4:30–6:30pm Daily 10pm–close Fri & Sat 9:00–close Sun–Thurs
Food Deals 2	$2.50 Fish tacos, cheesy poofs, soup, rasta rings, nachos, pot stickers, cactus enchilada, garlic fries
Drink Specials 3	$3.75 rum drinks (over 100 of them!) $4.00 red and white sangrias
Atmosphere 3	Fun tropical-themed-to-the hilt; Tsunami Rum Bar with unending and fascinating island decor!
	Other location: 1523 SW Sunset Blvd. 503/293-1790

8

Hawthorne

5008 SE Hawthorne
(503) 232-6333
www.thesapphirehotel.com

Sapphire Hotel

Happy Hours	4:00pm–6:00pm Daily
Food Deals 2	$5.00–$10.00 Humungo delicious salads: spinach strawberry, Thai caesar, citrus walnut; cheese, antipasta, and Mediterranean platters
Drink Specials 2	$1.00 PBRs $3.00 well drinks $4.00 selected wine $5.00 nightly drink special
Atmosphere 3	Mysteriously sexy and intriguing; Trés swanky! Intimate creative lounge decor. Ex-brothel! Outdoor sidewalk seating.

9

Downtown
(East Map)

214 SW Broadway
(503) 241-3393
www.saucebox.com

Saucebox

Happy Hours 4:30–6:30pm Tues–Sat

Food Deals 3 $1.00–$4.00
Asian-inspired fusion dishes: peanut noodles, satay, pad thai, salad and springs rolls, edamame, tataki (rare ahi), beed salad, fries, miso soup, great burgers!

Drink Specials 2 $2.50 Sapporo beers (small)
$5.00 daily cocktail
$5.00 & $6.00 wine
$4.00 Ocean Pacific special

Atmosphere 3 Big & open, boxy, saucy lounge; chocolate browns and greys; looming giant art murals lend more personality to entire room.

9

NW/Nob Hill

2112 NW Kearney
(503) 221-1195
www.serratto.com

Serratto

Happy Hours 5:00–6:30pm Daily

Food Deals 3 $3.00–$6.00
13 stellar menu items: stone oven pizzas (YUM!!), ribs, fries, clams, rigatoni, flame-broiled burgers, salads, penne, calamari, soup

Drink Specials 2 $3.00 white wine
$4.00 red wine
$5.00 cocktail specials

Atmosphere 3 Happy Hour is in their more casual "Vineria" which is only slightly Italian in ambience, but extremely pleasant and even romantic.

Extra Info Parking available in their lot on NW Johnson (approx. $4)

4035 NE Marine Drive
(503) 281-5944

Sextant

Happy Hours EVERY hour is Happy Hour here! They change their specials daily and vary them monthly, but offer great deals on both food and drink all day/night long.

Food Deals 2 Food specials change daily—surprise yourself! More of a casual bar menu than upscale gourmet.

Drink Specials 2 $1.75 domestics & $3.00 micros are common featured specials

Atmosphere 3 Outside, drink in the sunset as you enjoy your boat drinks on this prime-positioned wood deck. Inside is more of a smoky, only somewhat nautical, neighborhood watering hole.

7

Old Town

211 SW Ankeny
(503) 220-4001
www.shanghaitunnel.com

Shanghai Tunnel

Happy Hours	5:00–7:00pm Daily
Food Deals 3	$2.00–$6.00 Best pot stickers ever; also quesadillas, nachos, veggie burgers, chuck burgers, spuds
Drink Specials 2	$1.00 off draft beers (good list!) $1.00 PBRs $1.00 off wells
Atmosphere 2	Ghosts! Built over the underground Shanghai tunnels; upstairs has original painted murals and Asian-inspired simple touches. Seasonal outdoor seating.

9

Waterfront

909 N. Hayden Island Drive
(503) 283-4466

Shenanigans

Happy Hours	4:00–6:00pm Mon–Fri 4:00–8:00pm Fridays
Food Deals 3	$2.25–$3.95 Burgers, prime rib tortilla, wings, pasta, 1/2 club sandwich, Caesar, salmon cakes, quesadilla, skins
Drink Specials 3	$2.75 domestic drafts $3.50 house wines $3.50 wells
Atmosphere 3	Highest rating due to beautiful view along the Columbia! Inside, their "Tuxedo Charley's" bar has a large-screen, hi-def TV in the lounge area with movie posters encircling the modern-day, '70s Vegas-style hotel bar.

10

Alberta

2703 NE Alberta
(503) 922-3675
www.siamsociety.com

Siam Society

Happy Hours 4:00–6:00pm Mon–Fri
9:00–close Mon–Thur
10:00pm–close Fri & Sat

Food Deals 3 $1.75–$7.50
Extreme delicious-ness in Thai Happy Hour food! Cabbage wraps, grilled prawns, satay, spring rolls, ginger & tom yum soups, pad thai

Drink Specials 3 $2.50 draft beers
$3.50 wells
$4.00 house wine

Atmosphere 3 Big city award-winning design in lofty old power station; one of the coolest looks in Portland!

Extra Info Nice back outdoor beer garden but not available for HH patrons.

5

Belmont Area

533 SE Grand Ave.
(503) 230-7767
www.slowbar.net

Slow Bar

Happy Hours	3:00–6:00pm Mon–Fri
Food Deals 2	$2.50–$5.50 Pizzetta, green salad, mixed nuts, fries, ceviche, Southern fry
Drink Specials 2	$1.00 off all beers $2.50 well drinks
Atmosphere 1	Dark and smoky, laid-back popular hipster scene; all black; group seating at window.

"Draft beer, not people."

– Author Unknown –

9

Pearl

1300 NW Lovejoy
(503) 220-0080
www.solobar.net

SoLo

Happy Hours 11:00am–6:00pm Mon–Sat
10:00pm–close Mon–Sat

Food Deals 3 $2.50–$5.50 (1/2 off)
Phyllo wrapped brie, bruchetta, burger trio w/fries, escargot, veggie tempura, prawn and crab; $7.00 appetizer mix tray

Drink Specials 2 $1.00 off tap beer
$6.00 delicious infusion drinks
Plus revolving nightly discounts

Atmosphere 3 VERY well-designed industrial chic that takes the cement, rivots, and metal work to a new level. Fountains, curves, arches and flaming torches highlight all essential feng shui elements. Don't miss the cool bathroom!!

2808 NE MLK Blvd.
(503) 493-8127
www.billyreeds.com

Spice

Happy Hours 3:30–6:30pm Daily
11:00pm–1:00am Fri & Sat

Food Deals 2 $2.50–$4.25
Spiced-up bar-style standards: quesadillas, wings, nachos, ravioli, pasta primavera, burger

Drink Specials 2 $1.00 off beer
$1.00 off house wine
$3.50 well drinks

Atmosphere 2 The old Billy Reed's toned down; understated and low-key; wood and cement industrial; two very plush lounge rooms.

Belmont Area

1403 SE Belmont St
(503) 335-0811
www.stanfords.com

Squeez

Happy Hours 3:00–6:00pm Daily
9:00pm–close Sun–Thurs
10:00pm–close Fri–Sat

Food Deals 2 $2.95
Limited basic bar offerings: quesadillas, spring rolls, hot wings, chips & salsa, pot stickers, fries. Also pizza at all times.

Drink Specials 2 $2.75 micros
$2.75 well drinks

Atmosphere 1 Cool bar area with wild mosaic and mural art work, but theme goes more to a divey side; some reggae influence but more Kingston than Ocho Rios resort. Can be loud.

6

Lloyd Center-ish

913 Lloyd Center
(503) 335-0811
www.stanfords.com

Stanford's

Happy Hours 3:00–6:00pm Daily
9:00pm–close Sun–Thurs
10:00pm–close Fri–Sat

Food Deals 3 $1.95–$3.95
15 varied menu items including Southwest chopped salad, soup, BBQ chicken quesadilla, wings, crabcakes, pasta, burgers

Drink Specials 0 No drink specials

Atmosphere 3 Another Pacific Coast restaurant; the basic yuppie dark woods and hunter green look; upscale.

Other Locations:
1831 SW River Drive
(503) 241-5051

1440 N. Jantzen Beach Center
(503) 285-2005

0315 SW Montgomery (RiverPlace)
(503) 295-2747
www.thirstwinebar.com

Thirst

Happy Hours 3:00–6:00pm Tues–Fri
9:00pm–close Tues–Sun (food)

Food Deals 2 $1.50–$3.00
Offers a few nibbles good with wine: bruschetta, olives or cheese with bread, and crab dip

Drink Specials 2 $1.00 off red or white wine
$2.50 choice beers
$10.00 for the bartender's choice flight from 9:00–10:00pm

Atmosphere 3 Right on RiverPlace Esplanade with huge windows and sidewalk seating for people and river gazing; couch lounge area with fireplace. A truly enjoyable wine bar!

6

Old Town

71 SW 2nd Ave
(503) 222-2155
www.thirstylionpub.com

Thirsty Lion Pub

Happy Hours	4:00–7:00pm Mon–Fri
Food Deals 2	$1.95–$3.95 Ten pretty basic bar menu items: corn beef tacos, calamari, soup, garlic sautéed mushrooms, sliders, pub pretzel, sesame chicken
Drink Specials 1	Pint of the Day special
Atmosphere 2	A touch more sterile version of fun neighborhood English Pub, while being more yuppie/sporty with rockin' good-time atmosphere.

10

Waterfront

1510 SW Harbor Way
(503) 295-6166
www.threedegreesrestaurant.com

Three Degrees

Happy Hours 3:00–6:00pm Mon–Fri

Food Deals 3 $3.00
20 Gourmet-style selections; crab cakes, pumpkin ravioli, fondue, grilled prawn skewers, fresh salad selections, clams, sandwiches and burgers

Drink Specials 3 $3.00 martinis
$3.00 pints

Atmosphere 3 Romantic upscale perfection; river view with lots of windows; fireplace.

Extra Info Free valet parking! Can be crowded—can be empty—and service level will reflect this.

9

Alberta

1438 NE Alberta
(503) 288-6966

Tin Shed

Happy Hours	3:00–6:00pm Tues–Sun
Food Deals 3	$2.00–$4.00 Limited, but fresh and oh-so-tasty! Get the Jammin' Quesadilla! Southwest pasta, fish tacos, burger, salad, SW veggie pasta
Drink Specials 3	$1.75 domestic beers $2.75 microbrews $3.00 well drinks $5.00 specialty drinks
Atmosphere 2	Rustic corrugated tin walls; colorful & bright elsewhere. Loud interior; outdoor garden café with fireplace.
Extra Info	One of the best brunches in the city!

6

Pearl

1425 NW Glisan
(503) 221-1150
www.touchepdx.com

Touché

Happy Hours 4:00–6:30pm Daily

Food Deals 2 $2.00 gyros (chicken, lamb or veggie), $4.00 pizzas & Caesar, $5.00 Mediterranean platter

Drink Specials 2 $2.00 Miller beers
$3.00 wells
$5.00 cocktail of the day

Atmosphere 2 Semi-stately pool hall with grand staircase entrance and six nice full-size tables. Great for both trendy pool boys and true sharks.

Extra Info Outdoor wooden patio (but Happy Hour is upstairs in bar only)

10

NW/Nob Hill

120 NW 23rd Ave .
(503) 226-6909
www.uptownbilliards.com

Uptown Billiards Club

Happy Hours 4:00–7:00pm Tues–Sat

Food Deals 3 $10.00 (only for parties of 2–8) FIVE-course fine-dining experience! Menu is themed to a certain country and paired with select wines to match both the theme AND each course. Past presentations include "Spring in Chile" and "The Rain in Spain".

Drink Specials 3 $10.00 flight of wine; tastings are paired with each of five courses and are from the highlighted region

Atmosphere 3 Also totally different in the pool hall classification with its upscale class and elegance. Fancy, tucked-away billiards room. Non-smoking!

WOW!!! This Happy Hour is unparalleled elsewhere! Don't miss it! It's hands-down the BEST in my book!

9

Old Town

111 SW Ash
(503) 715-1798
www.voleurrestaurant.com

Voleur

Happy Hours	3:00–6:00pm Mon–Fri
Food Deals 3	$3.00 12 options including meal-size Sedona chicken wrap, buffalo burger, spinach & red pepper plus chicken quesadillas, panini, mac & cheese; plus fries, soup, salad, hummus, and satay
Drink Specials 3	$2.50 wells $2.50 pints (8 on draft)
Atmosphere 3	Soaring two-story arched windows with giant double-decker doors; large canvas original art; high wood beamed ceilings; pleasant turn-of-the-century Portland vibe.
Extra Info	Open 24 hours Fridays and Saturdays

10

Old Town

53 NW 1st Ave.
(503) 241-3840
www.voodoopdx.com

Voodoo Lounge

Happy Hours	5:00–7:00pm Tues–Sat 9:30–close Tues–Sat (food only)
Food Deals 3	$2.00–$5.00 Over 25 delicious choices! Jambalaya, bronzed rare ahi tuna, housemade sweet potato chips, singing pig farm salad, spring rolls and much, much more! Dee-lish!
Drink Specials 3	$3.00 tropical party drinks (15 island-style concoctions)
Atmosphere 3	Dramatic, moody, sexy interior; outdoor seating in New Orleans French-Quarter-style courtyard.
Extra Info	Check with bartender about Wednesday night buses to skiing, summer wake boarding and more.

9

Belmont Area

2411 SE Belmont
(503) 790-9090

Wild Abandon

Happy Hours	4:30–6:30pm Mon, Wed–Fri
Food Deals 2	$1.00–$6.00 Limited, but upscale offerings: soup, sautéed mushrooms, goat cheese torta, pasta, salads, mussels, burger, shrimp & polenta, chicken skewers
Drink Specials 3	$2.50 bottled beer $3.50 wine $3.50 sangria $3.75 wells Plus martinis & specialty cocktails
Atmosphere 3	Totally different on the inside than the out in more ways than one. The sweet, subdued “Red Velvet Lounge” has both indoor cozy dining plus a delightfully pleasant garden outdoor patio in back.

8

Old Town

15 SW 2nd Ave.
(503) 790-9090

XV

Happy Hours 4:00–7:00pm Daily

Food Deals 2 $2.00 off every food item
Big selection of good cheapies

Drink Specials 3 $2.50 pints
$3.00 wells
$4.00 wine
$5.00 specialty cocktails

Atmosphere 2 Black and more black; regular bar, but cool restaurant and candle-lit lounge in next room.

6

Alberta

2236 NE Alberta
(503) 284-1168
www.zaytoonbar.com

Zaytoon

Happy Hours	5:00–7:00pm Mon–Fri
Food Deals 2	$1.00 off Middle Eastern appetizers $2.00 off (low-priced) entrees
Drink Specials 0	No drink specials
Atmosphere 3	Minimalist hi-tech artsy with huge windows and soaring ceilings; seasonal outdoor sidewalk seating.

From Zaytoon's Website:

"True happiness arises, in the first place, from the enjoyment of one's self, and in the next, from the friendship and conversation of a few select companions."

– Joseph Addison

Bonus Section

This partial list below is courtesy of:
www.smokefreeoregon.com/directory/directory_portland.php

No Smoking Allowed

820 & Mint

Alameda Brew Pub

Alberta St. Pub

Amnesia Brewing

Andina

Aura

Bartini

Berbati's Pan

Bluehour

Bridgeport Brewing

Crush

County Cork

Crystal Ballroom

Dan & Louis'

Doug Fir Lounge

East

Echo

Empire Room

Green Papaya

H2O

Heathman

Hedge House

Henry's Tavern

Jo-Bar

Laurelwood Pub

Lucky Lab

Lucy's Table

MacTarnahan's Taproom

Madison's Grill

Manzana

McCormick & Schmick's

McMenamins

Newport Bay

Newport Seafood

Oba!

Old Town Pizza Co.

On Deck Sports

Pala Lounge

Portland City Grill

Portland Steak & Chophouse

Porto Terra

Pour Wine Bar

Rivers

Rock Bottom

Roots Organic Brewing

Salty's

Salvador Molly's

Sapphire Hotel

Serratto

Shenanigans

Stanford's

Three Degrees

Uptown Billiards

Vault Martini Bar

Voodoo Lounge

Wild Abandon

Dive Bar Dave's Fave Raves

Dave is a fictional character that loves a good "dive bar." Not that all the bars listed on these pages are truly divey per se, but they ARE ultra-casual, unpretentious bars where you can just hang out and kick back. Also, they pretty much have cheaper food & drinks at all times and have some great Happy Hours! Many people, guys in particular (and "Dave" especially), greatly prefer the low-key nature of the bars listed in these pages. Most are pretty smoky, and probably won't show up in any interior design magazines, but are nonetheless cool places to chill...

Ash Street Saloon
(Old Town Map)
225 SW Ash St
(503) 226-0430
ashstreetsaloon.com

4:00–8:00pm Mon–Fri
$2.50 menu items
$1.50 PBRs
$2.50 micros & wells

Sidewalk seating

Bar of the Gods
(Hawthorne Map)
4801 SE Hawthorne
(503) 232-2037

5:00–8:00pm Mon–Fri
$1.00 PBRs
$2.50 wells

Good back patio

Beulahland
(Lloyd Center Map)
118 NE 28th Ave.
(503) 235-2794

4:00–7:00 Daily
$1.00 off menu items
$3.00 pints & wells

Funky decked-out walls

Captain Ankeny's
(Old Town Map)
50 SW 3RD Ave
(503) 223-1375

1:30–7:00pm Mon–Fri
$3.00 wells

4:00–7:00pm Daily
Pizza & apps discounts
$3.00 micros

Sidewalk seating

Green Room
(NW/Nob Hill Map)
2280 NW Thurman St
(503) 228-6178
www.grpub.net

4:00–7:00pm Daily
$3.00 BIG nachos, burgers, and BBQ sandwiches
$2.50 drafts & wells

Back patio; music or entertainment nightly

Gypsy
(NW/Nob Hill Map)
625 NW 21st Ave.
(503) 796-1859

4:00–6:30pm Mon–Fri
$1.95–$3.95 menu
$2.00 wells(!) & PBRs

The Velvet Lounge and bar side is quite swanky

Lotus Room
(Downtown East Map)
932 SW Third Ave
(503) 227-6185
conceptentertainment-
group.com

4:00–7:00pm Mon–Fri
$2.00–$5.00 appys
$2.50 domestics & wells

Huge bar and cool back card room; sidewalk seating

LaurelThirst Pub
(Lloyd Center Map)
2958 NE Glisan
(503) 232-1504

Before 5:00pm Mon–Fri
$3.00 micros

6:00–8:00pm
FREE live music

Sidewalk seating

Low Brow Lounge
(Pearl Map)
1036 NW Hoyt
(503) 226-0200

5:00–7:00pm Daily
$2.75 wells
$1.00 off taps beer

Dave's fave!

Rogue Brewery
(Pearl Map)
1339 NW Flanders St
(503) 222-5910
www.rogue.com

3:00–5:00pm Mon-Fri
10:00pm–close Mon-Fri
Cheap bar food discounts, but no drink specials

Rip roarin' rogue-y hang out; sidewalk seating

Space Room
(Hawthorne Map)
4800 SE Hawthorne
(503) 235-8303

Cheap & happy all the time
$3.00 wells

Blacklight UFO theme

Virginia Cafe
(Downtown West Map)
725 SW Park Ave.
(503) 227-0033

4:00–7:00pm Mon–Fri
Cheap bar-style eats
$2.50 domestics
$3.50 micros
Double-ups on wells

Cuter victorian upstairs; sidewalk seating

The Best o

These are some great places that don't discount their food, but are fun places to go for a drink!

Bink's
2715 NE Alberta
(503) 493-4430
4:30–6:30pm Mon–Fri
$2.50 micros;
$1.50 PBRs
Casual w/ Bohemian touches

Bonfire Lounge
2821 SE Stark
(503) 232-3704
4:00–7:00pm Daily
$1.00 off wells & micros
A vaguely dungeon-like, artsy, and fiery bar

I love it!

Brazen Bean
2075 NW Glisan
(503) 294-0636
5:00-8:00pm Daily
$4.00 martinis (25 unique!)
Charming, well-decorated old Victorian with several living rooms and cute porch

East
322 NW Everett
(503) 226-1569
5:00–9:00pm Mon–Fri
$2.00 wells;
1/2 priced drafts
VERY cool red light lounge, memorable & striking place!

Hedge House
3412 SE Division
(503) 235-2215
Tuesdays
$2 pints
Sweet old Victorian house with big outdoor porches

Drinks-Only Specials

Hobo's
120 NW 3rd Ave.
(503) 224-3285
4:00–7:00pm Mon–Fri
$1.00 off all beer,
wine & wells
Old-time stagecoach
Portland charm; over the
Shanghai Tunnels

Holocene
1001 SE Morrison
(503) 239-7639
www.holocene.org
5:00–8:00pm Wed–Fri
$1.50 PBRs
$3.00 microbrews
$2.50 wells
$4.50 cocktails
Cool nightclubby place

Lucky Lab Brewery
915 SE Hawthorne
(503) 517-4352
Tuesdays
$2 pints
Bring your dog to their
outdoor beer garden :)

Vault Martini
226 NW 12th Ave.
(503) 224-4909
4:00–7:00pm Mon–Fri
20+ martinis $4.00-$5.00
Trés cool martini lounge!

Wine Down on 28th
126 NE 28th Ave.
(503) 236-9463
Tuesdays
$2 pints (extra good beers!)
Wednesdays
$1.00 off wines
Nice upscale wine bar/
restaurant

Microbreweries

Alameda Brew Pub
4765 NE Fremont
(503) 460-9025
alamedabrewhouse.com

Amnesia Brewing
832 N. Beech
(503) 281-7708

Big Horn Brewing (RAM)
320 Oswego Point
(503) 697-8818
theram.com

BJ's
825 NE Weidler
(503) 288-0111
–and–
12105 North Center
(503) 289-5566
bjsbrewhouse.com

Bridgeport
1313 NW Marshall St.
(503) 241-3612
–and–
632 SE Hawthorne Blvd.
(503) 233-6540
bridgeportbrew.com

Full Sail Brewing Co.
0307 SW Montgomery St.
(503) 222-5343
fullsailbrewing.com

Laurelwood
1728 NE 40th Ave.
(503) 282-0622
–and–
2327 NW Kearney St.
(503) 228-5553
laurelwoodbrewpub.com

Lucky Labrador
915 SE Hawthorne
(503) 236-3555
–and–
1945 NW Quimby
(503) 517-4352
–and–
7675 SW Capitol Hwy.
(503) 244-2537
luckylab.com

Mashtun
2204 NE Alberta St.
(503) 548-4491

McMenamins
See pages 83-85.

McTarnahan's Taproom
2730 NW 31st Ave.
(503) 226-7623
macsbeer.com

Raccoon Lodge & Brew Pub
7424 SW Beaverton-Hillsdale Highway
(503) 296-0110
raclodge.com

Rock Bottom Brewery
210 SW Morrison
(503) 796-2739
www.rockbottom.com

Roots Organic Brewing
1520 SE Seventh Ave.
(503) 235-7668

Rogue Brewhouse
339 NW Flanders St.
(503) 222-5910

Tugboat Brewing Co.
711 SW Ankeny St.
(503) 226-2508

Widmer Brothers Brewing
929 N Russell St.
(503) 281-2437
widmer.com

Go for the beer!

County Cork
1329 NE Fremont St.
(503) 284-4805

104 beers on tap
Dublin Pub
6821 NW Beaverton-Hillside
(503) 297-2889

100 beers on tap
Henry's 12th Street Tavern
10 NW 12th Ave.
(503) 227-5320
henrystavern.com

Horse Brass Pub
4534 SE Belmont St.
(503) 232-2202
horsebrass.com

Moon and Sixpence
2014 NE 42nd Ave
(503) 288-7802

200+ bottled beers
Produce Row Cafe
204 SE Oak St.
(503) 232-8355
producerowcafe.com

Wine Bars

Carafe
200 SW Market
(503) 248-0004
carafebistro.com

Noble Rot
2724 SE Ankeny
(503) 233-1999
noblerotpdx.com

Pour Wine Bar
2755 NE Broadway
(503) 288-7687

Sip D'Vine
7887 SW Capitol Hwy.
(503) 977-9463
sipdvine.com

Southpark Seafood Grill & Wine Bar
901 SW Salmon
(503) 326-1300
southpark.citysearch.com

Thirst Wine Bar
315 SW Montgomery
(503) 295-2747
www.thirstwinebar.com

Urban Wine Works
407 NW 16th Ave.
(503) 226-9797
www.urbanwineworks.com

Vino Paradiso
417 NW 10th Ave.
(503) 295-9536
www.vinoparadiso.com

Vino Vixens
2929 SE Powell
(503) 231.VINO
(I LOVE the back room!!)

Wine Down on 28th
126 NE 28th Ave.
(503) 236-9463

Best-of Categories

Overall Favorites

My Personal Favorites

Aura

Basil Bar

Bartini

Dragonfish

Gilt Club

Jake's

La Calaca

Oba

Rivers

Salty's

Salvador Molly's

Sapphire Hotel

Serratto

Siam Society

The Ram (outside)

Three Degrees

Uptown Billiards

Voodoo Lounge

Most Widely-Mentioned Faves Overall

820

Heathman

Henry's

Jake's

McCormick&Schmick's

Oba

PDX Chophouse

Portland City Grill

The following is a "Best-of" listing by category:

Asian
Barcode
Basil Bar
Dragonfish
Green Papaya
Masu
Siam Society
Saucebox

Brewpubs
Alameda
Bridgeport
Henry's
McMenamins (all)
The RAM
Rock Bottom

Chicken Wings
Basil Bar
City Sports
Madison's
Muu-Muus

Classy Old-School
Driftwood Room
Heathman
Huber's
Jake's (both)
Mama Mia's
Ringside
Uptown Billiards

Cocktails
820
Alibi
Bartini
Brazen Bean
Jo-Bar
Vault
Voodoo Lounge

European-Style Pubs (and beer)
Alberta St. Pub
County Cork
Moon & Sixpence
Thirsty Lion

Family Friendly
Hedge House
Laurelwood(s)
Madison's
McMenamins (all)
Tin Shed

Funky Retro Vibe
Aalto
Basta's
Crush
Doug Fir
Pour

Hamburgers
Imbibe
Jake's (both)
Ringside
Saucebox
Serratto

Italian
Alessandro's
Ciao Vito
Mama Mia's
Sal's
Serratto

Later Happy Hours
Alberta St. (5-8)
Bettie Ford (5-9)
Bar Code (4-10)
H2O (4-8)
La Calaca (8-10)
Pala Lounge (7-9)

Latin Style
Colosso
Fernando's
La Calaca
Oba
Pambiche

Luscious Lounges
East
Gilt Club
Sapphire Hotel
Vault

Old Portland Saloons
Hobos
Mother's
Old Chicago Pizza
Rose & Raindrop
Voleur

Outdoor Patios with Charm
(with HH seating)
820
Bernie's
New Old Lompoc
Night Light
Perry's
Tin Shed
Voodoo Lounge
Wild Abandon

Outdoor Sidewalk Dining
(with HH seating)
Basta's
Berbati's Pan
Blue Hour
Jake's Famous
Jo-Bar
Manzana's
Oba
Rock Bottom
Shanghai Tunnel
XV

Outdoor River Views
(with HH seating)
The Ram
Salty's
Sextant
Shenanigan's
Thirst

Pizza
Alessandro's
($2 whole cheese)

Old Town Pizza
($1 slice after 9)

Serratto
(stone ovens)

Pool Tables
Henry's
Hobo's
Madison's (free!)
Rialto
Ringlers (McMenamins)
Rock Bottom
Touché
Uptown Billiards

Seafood
Dan & Louis' Oyster Bar
Jake's (both)
Newport Bay
Newport Seafood
Salty's

Southern Cooking
Bernie's
Roux
Voodoo Lounge
Rose & Raindrop

Sports Bars
The City
Macadams
McFadden's
On Deck
The Ram

Tropical Get-aways
Alibi
Beaches
La Calaca
Pambiche
Salvador Molly's

Unique Interiors
Alibi
East
La Calaca
Siam Society
SoLo

Visitor Showpieces
Bridgeport Brewery
Edgefield's
Kennedy School
Henry's
Jake's
Portland City Grill
Salty's

Winter Night Havens
Alberta Public House
Blue Moon's Fireplace Table
Heathman (Tea Court Room)
Ringside

About the Author

Cindy Anderson is a self-proclaimed Happy Hour Expert who realized that the people of Portland needed a convenient and reliable source to help find the best deals in the city. She blended her talents as a graphic designer and artist, stirred in her Happy Hour expertise and desire to bring joy to the world, ate and drank 'til the cows came home, and created this wonderful concoction known as the *Happy Hour Guidebook.* Originally from Chicago (where they don't have Happy Hours, as most cities don't), she moved to Portland in 2004 and LOVES it! This is her first book.

Cindy loves Happy Hours and the pursuit of happiness, traveling, hiking, skiing, party buses, Jimmy Buffett, naps, golfing, reading, painting, and all things Tiki. She also enjoys road-tripping, pub crawling and gallery hopping; mojitos, Margaritas and microbrews; imports, good wine, and just about everything that involves meeting up with a friend or two and having fun!

Check our website for updates on restaurants, Happy Hour schedules, new bar openings, closings, and other important and fun info!

www.happyhourguidebook.com

"It's 5 o'clock somewhere."

– Alan Jackson & Jimmy Buffett –